HOCKEY
STRONG

HOCKEY STRONG

STORIES OF SACRIFICE FROM INSIDE THE NHL

TODD SMITH

GALLERY BOOKS
New York
London
Toronto
Sydney
New Delhi

FOR MURPHY

G

Gallery Books
An Imprint of Simon & Schuster, Inc.
1230 Avenue of the Americas
New York, NY 10020

First Gallery Books paperback edition May 2017

GALLERY BOOKS and colophon are registered trademarks of Simon & Schuster, Inc.

For information about special discounts for bulk purchases, please contact Simon &
Schuster Special Sales at 1-866-506-1949 or business@simonandschuster.com.

The Simon & Schuster Speakers Bureau can bring authors to your live event. For more
information, or to book an event, contact the Simon & Schuster Speakers Bureau at
1-866-248-3049 or visit our website at www.simonspeakers.com.

Interior design by Jaime Putorti

Manufactured in the United States of America

10 9 8 7 6 5 4 3 2 1

Library of Congress Cataloging-in-Publication Data is available.

ISBN 978-1-5011-1834-0
ISBN 978-1-5011-5723-3 (pbk)
ISBN 978-1-5011-1837-1 (ebook)

CONTENTS

GLOSSARY

Agitator: a player with an aggressive playing style who deliberately tries to frustrate an opponent with hits, fights, stick work, and insults in an attempt to take them off their game. Example: David Clarkson.

American Hockey League (AHL): minor league hockey organization that is the NHL's main development league.

Battle of Alberta: historic rivalry between the Edmonton Oilers and the Calgary Flames.

Beer League: a recreational hockey league for adults who are well past their prime. Example: author Todd Smith.

Bench Clear: a massive hockey scrum where all the players leave the bench to fight.

Big Bad Bruins: nickname of the Boston Bruins hockey club from the 1960s through the 1980s because of their relentless pugilism.

Bloody Wednesday: a violent and tide-turning game between the Detroit Red Wings and the Colorado Avalanche on March 26, 1997, at Joe Louis Arena in Detroit, Michigan.

Bus League: minor league hockey where bus travel is the primary mode of transportation.

Call-up: a promotion from the minor leagues to the NHL.

Captain: a leader designated by the team because of their work ethic, skill, perseverance, and mental and physical strength; wears the letter C on the front of his jersey. Example: Steve Yzerman. Alternate captains wear the letter A on their jerseys.

Cheap Shot: a borderline legal play that is often an attempt to injure an opponent.

Checking Line: a third or fourth line on a team deployed to play solid defense against (and irritate) an opponent's top offensive talent. Example: the Crash Line.

Chiclets: teeth ("I got cross-checked in the face by Kevin Hatcher and he knocked out four front teeth. The trainer had to scoop my Chiclets out of my mouth guard," said Paul Ranheim).

Chirp: a constant stream of smack talk ("I don't think you can have a handlebar mustache if you're four foot two," Shawn Thornton, then of the Boston Bruins, said to a diminutive Montreal forward).

Cornerman: a hardworking player skilled in the act of digging the puck out from the corners of the ice and holding off opponents. Example: J. P. Parise.

Crash Line: nickname for the New Jersey Devils' rampaging fourth line of Bobby Holik, Randy McKay, and Mike Peluso.

Cup of Coffee: a call-up from the minor leagues to the NHL that lasts only a short time ("I got called up from Albany to the big club but only stayed long enough for a cup of coffee before they sent my ass back down").

Dirty: a playing style or action that is dangerous, disruptive, and oftentimes illegal.

Drop the Gloves: when a player sheds his hockey gloves and drops them to the ice to fight.

Enforcer: the mean guy at the end of the bench who protects the star player.

Face Wash: the act of rubbing the smelly palm of a hockey glove in an opponent's face usually during or after the whistle scrum.

Finishing a Check: a player who fully commits to hitting an opponent and does not pull up even if the opponent no longer has the puck or is not immediately involved with the play. Example: Kirk Maltby.

Flow: a nice crop of hair that flows out of the helmet.

Forecheck: to skate hard into the offensive zone and body-check the opponent who has the puck in an attempt to force a turnover.

Gary Smith: an American-born athletic trainer who was the head trainer for the 1980 "Miracle on Ice." Also the author's storytellin' dad.

Gong Show: an absurd amount of craziness, violence, or debauchery that occurs either on the ice or off the ice.

Goon: a player with limited skills whose primary role is to intimidate and fight. Example: Stu Grimson.

Gordie Howe Hat Trick: slang term for when a player records a goal, an assist, and a fight in one game; named after the hockey legend who was renowned for his balance of offensive skills and physical play. Example: Rick Tocchet.

Grim Reaper: Stu Grimson, a particularly powerful Canadian hockey enforcer.

Grind Line: nickname for the infamous Detroit Red Wings fourth line of Kris Draper, Kirk Maltby, and Joe Kocur (and later Darren McCarty), because of their ability to wear down their opponents with physical play, fighting, and obscenities.

Heavyweight: title for the most fearsome fighter in a hockey league. Example: Dave Brown.

Herbies: a notorious and punishing skating exercise named after its main progenitor, Coach Herb Brooks.

High Motor: a player who possesses a relentless and hustling playing style, never taking a shift off and coasting. Example: Zach Parise.

International Hockey League (IHL): a defunct minor hockey league.

Iron Range: an area in northern Minnesota known for its picturesque wilderness, blue-collar towns, and penchant for producing tough hockey players. The "Range" is a hockey hotbed and is the home of the Carlson Brothers, the real-life inspiration for the movie *Slap Shot.*

Jam: a bullish style of play along the boards and in front of the net. Example: Charlie Coyle.

Journeyman: a player who moves from team to team but is valued for a specific skill set and character. Example: Craig Berube.

Juniors: amateur hockey in North America for players ages sixteen to twenty.

Knuckles: nickname for Chris Nilan, because of his willingness to chuck them.

Legion of Doom: nickname for the Philadelphia Flyers' high-scoring and imposing line of Eric Lindros, John LeClair, and Mikael Renberg during the 1990s.

Lunch-Bucket Player: a player who has a working-class playing style, one full of grit and tenacity, who figuratively punches the time clock and does his job willingly. Example: Darren McCarty.

Miracle on Ice: the monumental hockey game in which the United States upset the Soviet Union at the 1980 Winter Olympics in Lake Placid, New York. The U.S. team went on to defeat Finland and win the gold medal.

Mucker: a player who goes hard into the less desirable areas of the ice and relishes the battle. Example: Shjon Podein.

Old-Time Hockey: a bygone era of hockey from the 1940s to the 1980s that involved legendary players, lots of goals, hard-nosed players, and multiple fights. Example: Lou Nanne.

Orbital Bone: the bone around the cavity or socket of the skull in which the eye and its appendages are situated and which is often broken in fights.

Penalty: a timed punishment for a player infraction that may be either a minor penalty (small violation) or a major penalty (large and more serious violation).

Penalty Kill: playing shorthanded because one or more of your guys are in the penalty box and the other team has a power play; abbreviated PK.

Power Play: when a team has a man advantage due to the opponent's penalty.

Pylon: a stationary and useless hockey player.

Repairs: the fast treatment of a hockey injury.

Salad: hockey hair that is large and epic.

Sandpaper: an abrasive playing style meant to rub the player down.

Scrapper: an undersize player who never backs down from a challenge. Example: Chris Nilan.

Scrum: heated pushing and shoving between multiple players, typically seen in front of the net after the play has stopped. Example: the Grind Line.

***Slap Shot*:** a cult Hollywood movie from 1977 starring Paul Newman and featuring a fictional hockey team named the Charlestown Chiefs.

Taz: nickname for Boston Bruin forward Terry O'Reilly because of his wild, uncontrollable playing style, reminiscent of the Tasmanian Devil.

Todd Smith: author of the book *Hockey Strong*, and a Beer League pylon.

Upper-Body Injury: an intentionally vague medical term used to disguise a particular injury that could potentially be targeted by an opponent.

World Hockey Association (WHA): a defunct major hockey league that operated from 1972 to 1979.

Yard Sale: the appearance of the ice after a major brawl, where equipment and sticks and jerseys are strewn across the ice.

Zipper: a particularly gruesome line of stitches.

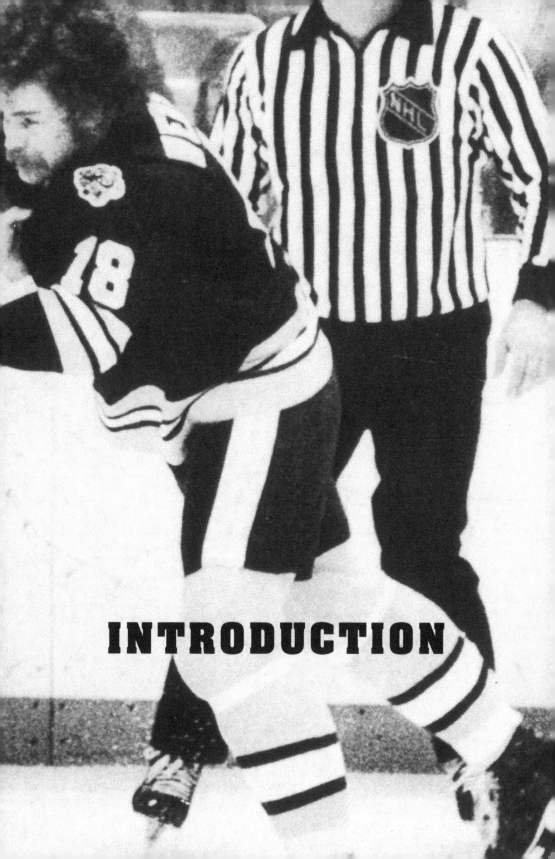

INTRODUCTION

What is your best scar story?"

It was a simple question I asked. But I knew the answer wouldn't be so simple; I was talking to Mike Rupp, after all, a grizzled and gregarious veteran of more than six hundred NHL games.

As he slowly took his pads off after a Minnesota Wild practice, Rupp took a few moments to respond, his brain flipping through a medical file of his numerous hockey nicks and cuts. He was a player who had battled long and hard through the trenches of the minor leagues and the NHL, and over his career had obtained enough stitches to make a baseball blush. Rupp didn't have to look too far for an amazing scar story: it was right there at the tip of his nose.

"I was playing in the American Hockey League and a scrum broke out," Rupp said. "An opponent came up from behind, put his glove over my nose, and gave a good tug."

But this was no standard face wash.

"He pulled part of my nostril off and it was just hanging there," Rupp said. "I went to the locker room and took twenty-nine stitches."

The wound Rupp suffered during that AHL game was just the beginning of the story about the scar on the end of his nose. That is because hockey scars are often much more than the mere traces of past sutures. Every hockey scar has its own unique story, its own origin in pain and circumstance. For the hockey player it is a permanent reminder of his sacrifice.

At the time Rupp had his nostril ripped off, he was literally fighting for a chance to play in the NHL. And so he got his nostril reattached and went back into the game and bravely fought the perpetrator, an act of courage that showed everyone on his team and the scouts watching in the NHL that his commitment and toughness were beyond question.

Years later, Rupp established himself in the NHL, where he provided solid veteran leadership throughout his long career. But he never forgot the nostril-tearing incident. When Rupp was playing for the Columbus Blue Jackets, the player who gave him the scar at the end of his nose joined the team.

"I turned the corner in the locker room one day and there he was. I saw him and had an instant hot flash that I was going to kill him," Rupp said, as he gave a chuckle. "But he was actually a pretty good guy. We hashed it out over lunch."

Lunch-enabled goodwill aside, scars and stitches and broken bones are simply a part of the game for NHL players. Between the body checking, boards, skates, puck, sticks, scrums, and fights, slight are the chances that a hockey player will leave the game unscathed.

So, what keeps them going? How do the players survive the near-constant assault on their bodies and minds? What does a player like Mike Rupp possess that allows him to go back into a game immediately after suffering such a gruesome injury?

Mike Rupp—and all hockey players, really—are hockey strong, and this means they possess an ancient athletic ethos that tells them they must try to play through pain. It is a black-and-blue doctrine that was born with the sport itself and guides players to this day through injury, agony, and fear, and out of the training room and back onto the ice. Since the beginning, NHL players have possessed unwavering mental and physical fortitude, a stamina that has been forged in each one of them over a lifetime of sacrifice in the sport. But being hockey strong is more than just physically possessing a high threshold for pain. Hockey strong is an untouchable and unbreakable spirit that is buried deep in its players, housed safely in a place of tradition and lore. The game's long and storied history of participants playing in pain flows through its veins and gives the sport its true pulse. Hockey may have one of the richest histories in professional sports, and the most magnificent trophy of them all in the Stanley Cup, but for all its climactic goals, saves, historic game sevens, and immaculate sweaters, the true lasting legacy of hockey, the one thing that simply can't be denied, the one thing that will never, in fact, die, is the toughness of its players.

During the course of writing this book, I set out to gather stories that exemplified what it means to be hockey strong.

My journey was both a professional and personal explora-
tion. Long before I was a journalist, I was a hockey player,
a rink rat in my native Minnesota. The inspiration for this
book came out of my own hockey scars, particularly the
eleven-stitch scar that splits my chin in half, the remnant of
a thunderous body check I both delivered and received during my otherwise unremarkable high school hockey career in
the Twin Cities.

During my playing heyday, I was at times battered and
cut and knocked out cold. Now I'm forty-three years old,
and I still play (and I'm still terrible). For a long time I hadn't
accorded much significance to any of the hockey injuries that
I sustained over my life. I didn't think anything of them. They
were just a part of the deal. You got cut, you got knocked
down, you lost blood, you broke a bone. No big deal. But I was
shaving one night and staring at my ugly mug in the mirror
and noticed how the scar tissue on my chin from my years as
a hockey player didn't allow my beard to grow in fully, and in
that moment the idea for this book was born.

Standing there at my bathroom sink, I took a look at my
own hockey scar and vividly remembered every detail of hitting a player twice my size straight-on, my world going black,
and waking up in the locker room with firecrackers going off
in my brain. I remember vomiting at home because of the
excruciating pain due to a serious concussion. I remember my
mom taking me to the emergency room to get evaluated, CT
scanned, and stitched up.

After I recovered from my concussion, I kept playing. Sometime later, I severely wrenched my shoulder during a game and was unable to lift my arm past my waist. As a result I wore a mobile electrical stimulation machine (known as an E-Stim machine) attached to my belt and electro-pads hooked to my shoulder underneath my school uniform. I went to school for an entire week like that: not being able to lift my arm, gutting it out in practice, and having electricity spastically shot into my shoulder, all so I could play in meaningless junior varsity games in ugly, industrial-looking arenas that were used as tornado shelters in the summer.

As a fully grown man, I stared at my own hockey scars and asked myself why I would have done that when I was sixteen. Why was I that committed? Why did I care that much, even though I was nothing more than a fourth-line plugger on the junior varsity with absolutely no hope of going anywhere with my hockey skills?

After talking to the NHL players featured in this book, I now know why. It was because there was something buried deep inside me—and inside all hockey players, regardless of skill level—that guided me. I instinctively knew that I should try everything I could to keep playing. It didn't matter that I was short and slow and terrible. What mattered was that I was a hockey player, a Minnesotan, and I was a part of something bigger than me, and that something was an ancient tradition of players playing in pain. I wasn't a baseball player. I wasn't a basketball player. I was a hockey player, and in our culture the players play in pain. That's just what we do. So, I played on.

From the very inception of the game, possessing hockey strength wasn't optional. This is because hockey wasn't invented on some cozy court with a peach basket as a target or on a sun-splashed field with a gentle breeze, but rather was born during a sadistic Canadian winter where you could die or get seriously injured if you spent too much time outside. From the game's earliest origins, learning to play hockey wasn't as easy as learning to play other sports. It's not as easy as going into the driveway and just simply shooting some hoops or going into the front yard to play catch. Hockey is not a game of H-O-R-S-E. That is not a slam on other sports, either. It's just the reality. There is an element of survival, both mental and physical, in hockey—taken to its sublime peak in the NHL playoffs—that you just don't find in other sports.

When a child first learns how to play hockey, they must learn how to suffer, how to survive the elements, and how to build up a pain tolerance before they can even learn how to handle a puck. Heck, before you even get to play or skate there's labor involved: the shoveling of the ice. Once a kid learns how to suffer, how to handle the elements, how to stare down icy winds with teeth, then everything else falls in line: skating, stick handling, passing, shooting, and hitting. That process is largely unchanged in the modern era of ice hockey. One of the most crucial aspects of the learning process is still how to stoke your internal boiler and build the desire to go back out there another day, because out there in the dark and cold, in the dead of winter, hockey strength is the only thing that truly grows.

Being hockey strong and having all the toughness that implies was a trait embedded in the DNA of the first players and provided the template for all the players to follow. Over time, being hockey strong has become a tangible life force, a rich culture that is silently transplanted into new players. It has crossed generations, continents, oceans, and every conceivable social and economic barrier. It continues to shape players so that when they are hurt, they try to gut it out for their teammates, for their team, for their family, for their town, and for their country. From the stark outposts of Russia to the wintry hinterlands of Finland to the brick streets of Charlestown, Massachusetts, to the frigid outdoor ice of Roseau, Minnesota, to towns in every far-flung Canadian province, no one hardly has to say a word to an injured hockey player, because this thread of toughness, this hockey heart, is inside them, alive and pounding.

All the players featured in this book demonstrate hockey strong. They span many eras and playing styles; there are fighters and pacifists and checkers and goal scorers. But regardless of when they played or the career stats they piled up, they all had one thing in common: toughness. Consider two players featured in this book: Lou Nanne, an old-time hockey stalwart who played for the Minnesota North Stars in the helmetless NHL rodeo days of the 1970s, and Charlie Coyle, a modern-day power forward for the Minnesota Wild, the sort of new-age dude who does hot yoga during the offseason.

Nanne and Coyle are two completely different players, from two very different eras, who have played professional hockey in the same state. But even though their playing careers are separated by forty-five years, they have the same mentality about serious injuries. Nanne had it when he played for weeks with a grotesquely torn elbow, and Coyle showed it recently when he played in the NHL playoffs despite a separated shoulder. Both men played on without any hesitation.

"You wanted guys to know that you were willing to play through pain," said Nanne. "When you got hurt, it was just a matter of were you able to function. It was something you grew up with. A trait that everyone had that played the game."

"Everyone is in a similar boat," said Coyle, echoing Nanne. "You can't sit around and say I have this or I have that. You can't make excuses."

Athletes not making excuses and instead gutting it out is, of course, nothing new. The sports world is filled with inspirational stories about injured athletes and how they have overcome adversity. We see moments of grit and toughness in other realms of the sporting world all the time: the fireplug Kerri Strug and her one-legged Olympic vault at the 1996 Summer Olympics; Curt Schilling and his stitched-up tendon and bloody sock in the 2004 American League Championship Series; Kirk Gibson tagging an epic homer on two busted legs and with a nasty stomach virus in Game 1 of the 1988 World Series; Willis Reed hobbling out with a torn muscle in his thigh in the 1970 NBA Finals; Jack Youngblood playing in the 1979 NFL playoffs, including Super Bowl XIV, with a snapped fibula; Carli Lloyd being cut from the United States soccer team in her twenties only to drive harder, practice longer, to mentally and physical steel herself to try to make the U.S. national team again, and eventually become a golden-booted World Cup hero. You can find gutty and insanely tough performances in every sport, certainly including, besides the above, mixed martial arts, boxing, and rugby.

What separates a hockey player's toughness from other athletes' is the fact that being hockey strong is more than a single performance or bout or game or series or Olympics. Hockey strong is a way of life.

It begins with all the bitterly cold outdoor skating of a player's youth, the endless hours at the park or pond or backyard when the pain and frostbite settles in their tissue and bones and hardens them for the brutality ahead. Next, it is seen in the bleary eyes of the young player who is roused awake for her early morning practice. The young child begrudgingly peels back all the layers of comfort and warmth in bed and enters a dark predawn world where the frigid cold shakes her to consciousness in a shivering state. Then she is greeted by an ice arena that is illuminated with a harsh aluminum glow. And this happens every weekend for years on end. If the player is good enough, they'll then play in the amateur junior leagues of North America or in college, and if they're truly, *exceptionally* good, they will have to leave everything behind, including their families, to chase an NHL dream as thin as a wisp of snow in the sun. If they succeed there and are drafted by an NHL organization, they are rewarded with an even longer and tougher road through the minor leagues, with players going up and down, back and forth from the farm club to the NHL, an exhausting journey on the ladder to success. But they keep playing hard at every level because of their love of the game and their unrelenting hockey strength.

In the end, all of it—all the sweat and cold and early morning practices, all the long bus rides, all the heartbreak, all the continuous physical and mental sacrifice—provides every NHL player with a foundation of commitment unlike any other in the world of sports. Because of all that they have endured before skating a single minute in the NHL, hockey players will repeatedly play through astonishing levels of pain without question, because pain is all they've ever known.

The pain is inevitable, too. They all know it, because there is no hiding from it. Injuries and heartbreak and adversity become part of a hockey player's day-to-day existence. By the time a player makes it to the NHL, he has already suffered a litany of wounds and now has an intimate relationship with sacrifice. What's remarkable is that players typically just shrug it all off. Having a part of your nose ripped off would be a monumental, life-altering event for most people, including athletes. A hockey player, though, just gets back into the game because it is his instinct to do so.

Male and female players all over the world tell the story of hockey on their very bodies. It is sewn into them in countless stitches and set in casts and pressed upon them in bags of ice to heal the welts and bruises that spot their limbs like on a leopard. This history is in the scar above Shjon Podein's eye that is the mark left by a cut that took seventy-seven stitches to close; it is in the entire row of missing teeth in Craig Berube's mouth, a gaping memento from a thousand games of trench warfare in the league; and it is in the battering ram of a right hand of Detroit's Joe Kocur. A heritage of sacrifice is bludgeoned into them; indeed, it often breaks their very bones, as in the hit Kris Draper suffered in 1996 against Colorado that not only broke his entire face but also turned out to be the spark that ignited one of the best and bloodiest rivalries in the history of the league, between the Red Wings and Avalanche; it's in Kirk Maltby's foot, battered from taking slap shots off the toe of his skate while he was on the penalty kill; it is in Chris Nilan's fists from fighting his way through the league, repeatedly hammering his hands into helmets and faces only to get up and do it again the next game; and it's in Tampa Bay Lightning supersniper Steven Stamkos, who despite being a number-one draft pick and a goal-scoring juggernaut played immediately after having his nose smeared across his face by a Johnny Boychuk slap shot in 2011, returning to the game with giant wads of gauze shoved in his nostrils and dark storm clouds rapidly swelling under his eyes.

The pain and injuries and black eyes are not a macho thing, and no attention is to be drawn to them, either. (As expected, Stamkos simply returned unheralded to the bench with a new full face mask attached to his helmet and nothing was made of it.) The pain isn't glamorous. There's no preening and puffing up like a peacock for attention. It is more of a shut-your-mouth kind of thing. The pain is to be stretched out and treated in early morning and late-night therapy sessions. Treatment and rehab plans aren't open to the public or reporters, and they are conducted in the bowels of empty arenas in cold, cinder-block rooms warmed only by the mentholated burn of Bengay. An odor of swampy ball sweat and damp hot pads—pulled out of a stinking steamer with giant tongs—hangs in the air. There are training tables lined up in rows, with a player on each one suffering in his own unique way, a triage unit of banged-up wingers and defensemen, freshly stitched and toothless and aching and cursing and trying to be put back together one piece at a time.

They do this because unlike, say, the NFL, in which a player usually has six full days of recovery time between games, the NHL has an 82-game season, and that means games are played nearly every other night. There are trainers nicknamed Smitty and Worley with kung fu–strong hands and a disinclination to mince words during treatment, instead giving it to the players straight up while treating them with crippling, numbing ice and torturous stretching, all in an effort to keep the guys going. And they always keep going, playing through pain and honoring the ancient and unbreakable spirit that resides in them all.

"It's all hockey players," said Zach Parise, captain of the United States national team and forward for the Minnesota Wild. He should know. In the 2014–15 NHL season, Parise endured a massive cut on his face, and then months later had a tooth knocked out. But he refused to single himself out as anything special. He is a hockey player. Parise speaks the universal humble language of his sport. "It's just one of those things. You want to play. I got hit in the face. That's part of the game. It happens."

It happens a lot in hockey. This book is a testament to the strength and sacrifice it takes to play one of the world's toughest sports.

CHAPTER ONE
SHJON PODEIN

The Mayor of Muckerville sits on a stool in a suburban Minneapolis ice rink holding court. Shjon Podein is yucking it up and slapping backs. Great guffaws roll around deep inside him and then move up . . . up . . . up . . . and detonate in the rink lobby as he regales the hockey moms and dads around him with stories from his one-of-a-kind hockey odyssey.

During his decadelong career in the NHL, Podein was one of the most beloved third-line players. He was never the fastest or biggest or strongest or most gifted player on the four NHL teams he played for between 1992 and 2003, but he was tough, and hockey toughness comes in many shapes and forms. There are the fighters, of course, who practice the dark arts of the sport, punching and slashing and bashing and intimidating opponents. Then there are the players who battle through horrific injuries for the good of the team. Then there are the players like Podein, who are just extremely tough to play against.

For the entirety of his career, Podein was known as a sandpaper guy, a gritty player whose main job was to rub opponents down the hard way, doing everything he could to take the shine right out of their stars. He was up in the opponent's kitchen, their comfort zone, grabbing and sticking, scrumming, and chirping smack talk. Every team in the league has a player or an entire line whose whole goal is to make life miserable for the opponent's top line, hitting them at every turn, shift after shift. They're often anonymous players who are only appreciated by their hometown fans and are offhandedly referred to simply as grinders or plumbers or scrappers or, as in Podein's case, muckers. These third-line players toil in the hockey trenches, literally leaving skin in the game, and then they are gone, never to be heard from again.

What makes Podein the Mayor of Muckerville is that his turbulent and abrasive on-ice playing style was mixed with an off-ice personality that was equal parts Jeff Spicoli and Evel Knievel with a dash of *The Big Lebowski* sprinkled in for good measure. He was both a practical joker and a scrapper, a wild-eyed cartoon character with real-life wounds, a dude of the highest ilk who'll tell you that playing in 699 NHL games and winning the Stanley Cup with the Colorado Avalanche in 2001 were all nice, but what he's most proud of is his 25 Foundation, which he started to help sick kids.

Podein's career was a traveling circus of sorts that began in southern Minnesota and then hit the beaches of California, only to return to the Midwest, where he engaged in a one-man Cannonball Run, driving back and forth to play hockey at a college that initially didn't want him. His professional career started in the Edmonton Oilers' organization, where he yo-yoed back and forth between their minor league team in Nova Scotia and the Oilers in Alberta. Then Podein hit and scratched and clawed his way into a permanent roster spot in the NHL and stayed in the top league, including three full seasons with the Philadelphia Flyers. After becoming a forechecking folk hero in Philly he was traded to Colorado and won the Cup as a feral, bearded whirling dervish. He was beloved by fans and teammates for his stout work ethic and unrelenting willing-ness to go hard into the dirty areas of the ice rink. This led to multiple scars and injuries and getting tangled up with a slew of legendary NHL tough guys.

If you take a close look past Podein's jovial personality, you'll see that a third-line mucker like him doesn't leave the game unscathed. In his role, his body paid a heavy price, and he is deeply scarred. Some of the markings are clearly visible, and some are hidden on his face and mouth by a thick tuft of blond stubble. But each one of these scars has a story, and Podein is happy to oblige you with any of them.

"The curved scar over my left eye is from a wound cut so deep it reached my skull," Podein says as calmly as a man describing his grocery list. "There is a chipped tooth that's been repaired twice but kept on getting knocked out, so I said the hell with it and just left it chipped."

As Podein talks, ears perk up. Dads normally bored stiff by yet another youth sports practice stop scanning their cell phones for a second and listen to Podein as he revs up a story.

"Please don't bring up the time that big farm boy Jeff Beukeboom beat the living tar out of me," Podein says flatly. Then a thick laugh rolls out.

Two dads standing behind him in the lobby lean back and start hooting. Everyone loves Podes.

EVEN ON THIS RIPE summer day in the Twin Cities, the ice rink in suburban Minneapolis is full of skaters. The humid air outside is as thick as soup, and summer pummels its way inside, crushing the frigid rink air and fogging the lobby windows over. Podein's golf shirt, cargo shorts, and flip-flops are standard-issue dad apparel. He watches his seven-year-old son play hockey through both the lobby viewing windows and the Plexiglas around the rink, which gives the appearance that his son is playing hockey in an aquarium. Podein wipes away the fog on the viewing window and then applauds his son's efforts and waves at him at every turn. Every couple of minutes two large steel doors at the end of the ice rink lobby swing open, and the riotous summer squeals of the kids in the adjacent outdoor pool fill the lobby and laughter ricochets off the cold concrete walls. The doors slam shut, and in an instant the laughter is gone. In its wake is only the sound of pucks tink-tink-tinking off the Plexiglas.

At the end of a long drill, Podein's son slides up against the glass and waves at him again, a wide Cheshire-cat smile stretching out and over a chunk of mouth guard. As the son starts yet another skating drill, his smile recedes slowly. Podein feels it; he shrugs his shoulders because he knows all too well what it feels like to have your lungs burning out there on the ice.

"I know, son," Podein says sympathetically to himself as he gives his boy another wave of encouragement. "You've been doing line drills for forty-five minutes. I get it. I've been there."

Among the swirl of jerseys and cones and bleeping whistles Podein finds his son again and enthusiastically waves at him. It's not hard to spot Podein's son, either. Junior's the spitting image of his father, right down to the shock of blond hair, the wild-eyed gleam in his eyes, and the number 25 on the back of his uniform. Podein watches Junior burst through the drills, and gives no mind to the fact that he's the smallest player on the ice. In addition to the looks Junior inherited from his dad, he also got a healthy dose of the unrelenting hustle, drive, and reckless abandon that made Podes such a popular role player.

According to the elder Podein, when it comes to hockey, there is one striking difference between father and son.

"Junior is way tougher than I ever was," he says, chuckling, full of his usual good-natured self-deprecation. "I was a total baby as a kid."

As Podein begins to tell the story of his professional hockey career, he looks out toward the ice to gather himself, to find his bearings. The rink—any rink, in any city—has been his home for so long that it seems to ground him.

"I was blessed with a dad who taught me a strong work ethic," Podein says. He looks out toward the ice again and watches Junior Podein bang around in the corner like a racquetball and lets out a hearty laugh because of it. "So when things got tough, that's how I always trained. I embraced it."

Podein, a native of Rochester, Minnesota, was no star, a player with a straight-line trajectory into Division I hockey or the NHL. He was more of a rogue comet, hurling himself through every space on the ice and crashing into every opponent who came near him. Although Podein showed tremendous character and potential at Rochester's John Marshall High School, after graduation there were few offers.

From the very beginning, though, Podein didn't quit on a shift or on his dream of playing hockey. When his dream of playing at the University of Minnesota–Duluth died, he took an odd detour to the sunny beaches of Southern California.

"After high school hockey, I had a short stint playing hockey for the Soaring Sea Gulls at the United States International University in San Diego," Podein says. The Plexiglas in San Diego was forty feet high to keep the cool air near the ice, and the obscure hockey outpost, the team run by Minnesota native Brad Buetow, just didn't seem right.

"I didn't want to regret giving up on my dream of playing hockey at the University of Minnesota–Duluth," Podein says. "So I headed home."

There was only one problem: UMD still didn't want him. Podein lets out another loud chortle at the memory. Then he says, "UMD literally told me not to come. They told me that there was no room for me, so I shouldn't bother coming up there!"

Podein didn't listen and just went ahead and enrolled, unbowed and determined to play for the Bulldogs. He went to school Monday through Friday in Duluth. Then he started playing for the Rochester Mustangs of the USHL on weekends. His Mustangs coach, Frank Serratore, somehow convinced the UMD hockey program to let Podein practice with the team during the week.

"I was practicing with UMD, one of the best college programs in the country, during the week and playing in junior hockey on the weekends," Podein says with a righteous inflection. "How awesome is that?"

The Podein family didn't have a lot of money to fund his dream. So Shjon took matters into his own hands and bought a used 1978 Chevy Vega that had no heat, an AM-only radio, and a plastic Chicago Cubs helmet taped to the front. He drove the beast 230 miles back and forth between Rochester and Duluth every week.

"I'd get up at four a.m. on Monday morning and be in Duluth for my eight a.m. classes," Podein says. "I'd drive fifty-five miles per hour, try to stay out of the ditches, and listen to the *Sex Talk* radio show out of Chicago to stay awake."

All of those snowy miles and early-morning wake-up calls, and seven days of hockey per week, eventually paid off. He won a national championship with the Rochester Mustangs and through sheer force of will earned a spot on the UMD roster. He was put on the fourth line at Duluth and became a dependable, lunch-bucket type of player with a hot-running motor. By the end of his first season with the University of Minnesota–Duluth, Podein was drafted 166th overall by the Edmonton Oilers. In his third year in Duluth he scored 39 points in 35 games. After his junior year in college, Podein turned pro and reported to Cape Breton, the home of the Oilers' top minor-league affiliate in the American Hockey League.

Paths to the NHL aren't always pretty and smooth, like moves on a game board where a player slides easily from one team to the next, and always with upward mobility. There can be only so many players on the autobahn to the NHL; guys like Sidney Crosby and Patrick Kane ride straight into the bright lights. The road to the NHL for most players is filled with detours to the minor-league outposts of the AHL or the IHL, places such as Wheeling, West Virginia, to play for the Nailers or Milwaukee to play for the Admirals. During a player's time in the minor leagues, emotional and physical land mines can explode all around them, tearing apart their path and dreams with injuries, rejection, and failure.

This is a universal journey for players such as Podein, and it reminded me of a talk I had with Paul Ranheim about the same subject. Ranheim was raised in Edina, Minnesota, and after he retired from his long professional hockey career in the NHL he coached Minnesota high school hockey with Podein at St. Louis Park High School and currently coaches at Eden

Prairie High School, a hockey powerhouse in Minnesota. During the late 1980s, Ranheim was a collegiate all-American at the University of Wisconsin and a lofty second-round pick of the Calgary Flames. When Ranheim turned pro in 1988, the Flames were a stocked team, loaded with veterans who were dug into their roles and the lineup. More important, the Battle of Alberta between the Flames and the Edmonton Oilers was raging, and it was no place for a college kid to start his career. So the Flames sent the twenty-two-year-old Ranheim down to their IHL minor league affiliate, the Salt Lake Golden Eagles, in Utah.

"We bused to towns like Flint, Michigan, and Muskegon and Peoria, and it was a real mental test," Ranheim says. "We'd play three games in four nights. It'd be dreary out and miserable, and we'd pull into these towns in the middle of the night. You'd stare out the window and ask yourself, *How bad do I really want this?*"

"Nova Scotia was the true minor leagues," Podein says. "Last call at the bar Smooth Herman's was three forty-five in the morning. Everyone thinks pro hockey is like Zach Parise: ten million dollars a year. Between the taxes and finances and exchange rate and agent fees, I literally lost money playing professional hockey for the first year."

Life on the road in the NHL means that the team bus picks up the players at their swank hotel, with its five-star chef, Egyptian cotton sheets, and center-city locale, and then conveniently drops them off on the tarmac next to their chartered plane. In the minor leagues, though, the players get on the bus, and it doesn't stop until it gets to the next town. In the minor leagues, all the players, regardless of their skill level or draft selection, are literally on the same bus. Whether it's a mucker like Shjon Podein playing in Nova Scotia for the Cape Breton Oilers or a highly valued draft pick like Charlie Coyle playing in Houston for the Aeros or a former NCAA Hobey Baker Award finalist like Paul Ranheim doesn't matter. If you're in the minors, you're on the bus: veterans in the back, rookies up front, and pizzas delivered straight to the bus as it idles outside the arena after the game. Every player looks out the same window as the bus drives across the country into these minor-league towns that are stuck out on the margins of the sports world: there are the sun-scrubbed frontier towns out West, where hockey is nothing more than a circus attraction; there are the blue-collar towns of the Midwest, cities that have typically been pummeled by a failing economy and are now rusting carcasses of their former industrial selves; and there are the East Coast towns that are encased in concrete and shrouded in sheet-metal skies.

Ranheim remembers playing in ice rinks with names like the Corn Palace and the Salt Palace. These rinks were so far off the map, so far from the bright lights of Madison Square Garden, so far away from the buzzing metropolitan NHL hubs, that they were like islands in the South Pacific. Some of these arenas would have so few fans that an air of ambivalence hung over the game with enough weight to crush all the hopes and dreams in a player's heart, making him question his career choice and his future.

In the next game, Ranheim's team would enter a raucous bunker of an arena and play against an opponent and a town that treated the game like it was the last stand at the Alamo. Despite the shuttered factories and downturned economy, the town would be more than ready for the game at hand, each fan having circled it on his calendar with the finality of a death sentence. Each player knew he had to get up for the game, for the battle at hand, because it would all be on the line for their team and the town.

"We had a really tough team, too. Five guys with over two hundred penalty minutes. And we had Stu Grimson," Ranheim quips. "Oh boy, did we have some battles."

The hard times of daily life in these minor-league towns could be sensed in the rink on game night. It would be a Friday night in Peoria, Illinois. The beer would be cheap, served in tall wax-paper cups. The city's main employer, maybe a tire factory or an auto plant, would be struggling. There'd be rumors of layoffs, which felt like a noose being tied slowly around the whole town. But the fans would not think about any of that on game night. These minor-league fans had spent what little money they had for a slight reprieve, and they'd come to see their beloved Peoria Rivermen play. The fans paid for their tickets with their calluses, their square shoulders, their lives spent under hard hats, and would award themselves full license to berate the opponent. Through cupped fists and with pungent beer breath they would bark out words like "twat" and "fuckhole" as the visiting team came out onto the ice. Sometimes they would throw dead rodents onto the ice. They would bang the glass and pound drums and clang cowbells. And that'd just be in warm-ups.

After the game, regardless of the outcome, it would be back on the bus to the next town, to the next game, and to the next battle.

"Each bus ride was long enough to be uncomfortable but not long enough to let you sleep," Ranheim says. "We'd bus all night from Milwaukee to Indianapolis. I remember on that trip thinking that it was fall and football season and that I'd rather be home with my buddies watching a game. Then we pulled into our hotel, called the Knights Inn. I entered my room straight from the parking lot. I opened the door to my room, and the first thing I saw was purple velour sheets. It was disgusting. But we were all paying our dues."

Podein sympathizes with Ranheim's plight and lets out a riotous snort as he recalls his own "welcome to the minor leagues" moment. After a long road trip, the Cape Breton team pulled into the home arena, and Podein's car was up on blocks. Someone had taken the tires, which were worth more than the car.

"Podes just stood there not knowing what to do," Kirk Maltby, a Cape Breton teammate, says, laughing.

As Podein bounced back and forth between the minors and the luxurious big league, he needed more than just physical strength. He had to continuously stoke his inner fire and his love of the game, the same things that had fueled him on those drives between Rochester and Duluth. He remembered the '78 Vega; he remembered Duluth's initial rejection. So he kept plugging away, charging up that ladder to ring the big bell.

Every player in the minor leagues has to do this. They have to find their own personal way of getting up for the game at hand and the long road beyond it. AHL rosters are a mix of valued draft picks and retreads, of lifers and developing rookies, of Canadians and American college kids and European imports. And each one of these players is working inside this harsh unknown of what they have to do to get the call-up. A player can lead his team in points, like Ranheim did in Salt Lake City, and still not get the call. A player can routinely scrape with the toughest bastards in the minor leagues, game after game, like David Clarkson did in Albany, New York, and still not get the call. A player can grow into a power forward and be a bull below the goal line and in the corners and a sound player defensively, like Charlie Coyle in Houston, and still not get the call. But because they have worked so hard to get to that point, one rung below the NHL, they soldier forward.

"For a guy to get the call-up to the big club, so many things had to happen for him," Ranheim admits. "You would need luck, skill, timing, someone in your corner, and all of that has to come together."

But when a player finally gets the call-up to the big club, his journey is only just beginning.

"Once a player gets to the NHL, they have to find a way to *stick* in the NHL," Ranheim says.

Maybe the player stays up in the NHL for only a week or two. Maybe it's a month. They go from playing heavy minutes and being the league point leader in the AHL to being a healthy scratch for five games in a row in the NHL. If they make it into the starting lineup, maybe they play only sparingly and sit on the bench for long stretches, the sweat underneath their pads drying on their body, the chill a cold reality in more ways than one.

"It's such a difficult thing to make it in the NHL. Guys were always coming up. Guys were always going down," Ranheim says. "Guys were always thinking that they should be up there in the NHL. And when they were not there, it was a question of how did they react. Are they mentally strong enough? Is he going to fold? Or is he going to fight? There was always going to be players with more talent. But the mentally tough guys stuck in the NHL, and the weaker ones didn't."

PODEIN HAD MORE THAN enough motivation in his tank to get him through the slog of the American Hockey League. After several trips up and down between Cape Breton and Edmonton, Podein finally stuck in the NHL. And he had a helluva time doing it. During his numerous stints in Edmonton, longtime Oiler veteran Craig MacTavish was put in charge of him as a mentor.

"He was a godsend to me," Podein says. "I enjoyed life a little too much when I was younger."

Podein took to heart MacTavish's veteran wisdom and guidance. But that didn't mean he didn't have a little fun along the way. They were roommates on the road. After a lengthy road trip, Podein's brothers and his mom flew into town to visit. After the Podein brothers tucked their dear mom in for the night, things got a little wild.

"It was my twenty-fifth birthday," Podein says with a playful smirk.

They went out with the team, and at the end of the night Podein ended up in the hotel hallway wearing nothing but his underwear. It was dark out and he couldn't find his room. He resorted to going down numerous hallways and trying his key in random doors.

"For my birthday, my brothers had bought me a sombrero and a giant inflatable T. rex," Podein says. "A security guard comes up to me and says, 'I got a message about a guy in his underwear and a sombrero trying to get into rooms.' I looked the security guard dead in the eye and said, 'You got the wrong guy.'"

MacTavish was already in bed in Podein's room and was peacefully sleeping. So, Shjon took the opportunity to gently set the giant T. rex over MacTavish's head so the dinosaur was staring straight down at him. MacTavish, the hard-ass veteran hockey player who was still playing without a helmet, woke up in the middle of the night to find an angry dinosaur staring at him and started screaming.

Despite Podein's off-ice antics, MacTavish continued to mentor Podein throughout his up-and-down career with the Oilers. A few years later, MacTavish joined the Philadelphia Flyers and helped Podein sign with them as a free agent. This was a golden opportunity for Podein, because Philadelphia, and especially its sports fans, loves a good underdog.

Philly fans are notorious for booing Santa and chucking batteries at opposing teams. But they have a soft spot in their lunatic sports hearts for hard-charging, plucky scrappers, especially if they're undersized or underskilled but have the guts to take on all comers (for example, Rocky Balboa, Lenny Dykstra, Mo Cheeks, Allen Iverson, Charles Barkley, or Rick Tocchet). The Philadelphia Flyers, above all, embody the city's fighting spirit. Throughout their history in the league, what Flyer players lacked in talent they more than made up for in hustle and truculence. An opponent could have all the skills in the world, but the Flyers would just hit them in the mouth and then see what was what. Legendary Flyer captain Bobby Clarke summed up the Philly moxie best when he said, "We take the shortest route to the puck and arrive in ill humor."

When Podein landed with the Flyers, it was love at first forecheck. "That's when things really started for me," Podein says, reflecting on the moment he climbed all the way up to the NHL and stayed for good. "I got to Philly, and it was everything that I loved. The organization was all about winning, and it was blue-collar. I would walk out of a bar in South Philly and there would be dudes—straight out of the movie *Rocky*—yelling 'Yo! Podes!' It was just awesome."

At the time, the Flyers were the biggest team in league history, and they gobbled up every square inch of ice they could. The Legion of Doom line featured John LeClair, Eric Lindros, and Mikael Renberg and was one of the most feared trios in the 1990s. Podein held down the left wing on the third line, which was centered by a man-bear named Joel Otto, an Elk River, Minnesota, native who was hardened and ornery from spending many years in the Battle of Alberta, where he played shutdown center for the Calgary Flames and went nose to nose with Mark Messier of the Edmonton Oilers. The other winger on the line was Trent Klatt, another big-assed, corn-fed Minnesotan.

"Everyone called us the 3M Line, because we were all from Minnesota," Podein says. "But we called ourselves the 'I'm Sorry Line,' because after each shift we were saying that we were sorry to each other for our lack of ability."

As Podein developed into a first-class penalty killer, his body paid a heavy price; he was regularly deployed as a checking forward. He willingly gave up parts of his body for the good of the team; he was nicked for more than two hundred stitches and suffered multiple injuries that he played right through.

"I have a cut over my left eye," Podein says. "I was playing the Rangers in the playoffs. I got cut by Pat Verbeek. He tripped me and I went down and cut my head on the ice. When I got up I had no idea where I was. I looked at my jersey and saw that it was orange. I looked at Verbeek's jersey and saw that his was white. So I just went ahead and grabbed a white jersey."

The referees blew the whistle after the scrum, and Podein got to the bench. Flyers trainer John Worley came up and told Podein that he had to go to the locker room. Podein immediately said no, because he was a third-line guy and was ultimately afraid he'd lose his job. Then MacTavish, now a centerman on the Flyers, took a look at Podein's cut.

"MacTavish leaned over and told me that he could see my skull." Podein lets fly a buckshot of laughter. "That's when I got up and went to the locker room."

Podein points to a half-moon scar that cradles his left eye socket.

"So I went in to the locker room," Podein says. "I told the doctor that I was married and that I didn't care how I looked. Just get me back out there."

The doctor put five big stitches in to close the wound. Podein missed one shift.

"Later on, I went to a plastic surgeon," Podein says. "They did three levels of stitches, seventy-seven stitches around my eye. I didn't even know you could do that many."

Even after that horrific injury, Podein didn't stop sticking his nose into the battle zones. He had a grinder's appetite and took on everybody wearing the opposing jersey. Whether it was a star winger or a tough defenseman wasn't up for debate. Because of his pugnacity, Podein was involved in one scrum after another.

"Bob Probert was the toughest guy I ever faced," Podein says. "But Joey Kocur was end-your-career tough. The one story I heard about those two was that in the Red Wings' locker room, they used to set out the opposing team's lineup and they'd go over it and pick which guy they got to fight."

In one game, Podein got an up-close and personal introduction to Kocur.

"We were at a face-off together," Podein says. "Back in the day, you could pick guys and set screens. Kocur was going out to the point and I picked him. He wound up and punched me right in the back of the head. It really, really hurt. Then he said, 'What are you going to do about it?' I looked at him and said, 'Nothing, Mr. Kocur!'"

Podein retreated to the bench. All the guys on his team saw the whole thing happen and were giving him unsolicited advice.

"They all were saying to not fight him!" Podein says, his hands flying up like an evangelical preacher.

Podein's teammates knew he wasn't a pure fighter, and although he was a gamer, he wasn't exactly highly skilled in the art of chucking knuckles on ice. But they all knew he was just crazy enough to try his hand with the league's reigning heavyweight champ. Above all, Podes would do anything, especially if it would spark his team.

"They kept saying that I'd get hurt—like, *really* hurt."

While Podein wisely avoided engaging Kocur, he regularly answered the bell when he had to. The Beukeboom incident was an example of that. It was a typically nasty game between the Flyers and the Rangers. With the Flyers up 2–0 in the first period, the animosity reached a full, rolling boil, and Podein stepped in to meet the pressure. Right at the face-off he dropped the mitts with the Rangers' hulking defenseman Jeff Beukeboom. Joel Otto then went at it with Rangers center Mark Messier as they rekindled their hatred from their Battle of Alberta days. As Podein squared off with Beukeboom, he proceeded to get pounded.

At 6'5" and 240 pounds, Beukeboom was a lot to handle for any player, and Podein was overmatched. After throwing a flurry of punches and trading several big bombs, Podein performed an awesome Houdini act and wiggled free from Beukeboom's clutch. As he ducked out, Podein gracefully slipped straight into the protective arms of the linesman. Beukeboom grimaced in complete annoyance at Podein's magical escape from the fight.

As part of his role as a third-line player, Podein was required to play tough hockey in all areas of the ice. This often involved looking out for and protecting teammates who were being targeted. In one classic Podein move he stuck up for one of his teammates, Flyers star Eric Lindros, when the Florida Panthers' surly defenseman Ed Jovanovski viciously slashed him.

At the time, Lindros was not only one of the best players in the world; at 6'4" and 250 pounds, he could also handle himself in any fight. But that wasn't the point. He was the franchise, and didn't need to get into it. So Podein jumped into the fray to make sure Lindros didn't have to. As Lindros ended up in a tangled pile with Jovanovski and fell to the ice, Panthers veteran Dave Lowry intercepted Podein as he closed in to help Lindros. They clutched and grabbed and ended up trying to smash each other over the boards into the Panthers' bench. Soon a melee broke out, and all the players paired up; even the goalies got into it. Podein and Lowry were wrestling and punching when Podein ripped Lowry's jersey off.

After the fight was broken up, Lowry was still incensed and challenged Podein to fight again, because the referees quickly left them and were preoccupied with the large pile of players in the center of the ice. Because Lowry didn't have a jersey on, Podein did the honorable thing and removed his own so that Lowry wouldn't have a disadvantage. Podein tossed the jersey aside, and the two locked up again in their pads. Paul Laus, the Panthers' enforcer, saw what was happening and quickly jumped in. A dogpile ensued, after which Podein was escorted off the ice, but during his grand exit the entire Flyers bench stood up and applauded him for his efforts.

"Lowry shit-kicked me, just like most everyone else did," Podein says now.

Podein played five seasons and more than three hundred games with the Flyers, including their run to the Stanley Cup Finals in 1997, which they lost to the Detroit Red Wings. In 1998, in an effort to increase scoring, the Flyers traded Podein to the Colorado Avalanche for Keith Jones. Although Podein was heartbroken to leave Philadelphia, he stepped right onto another team that was prepared to make deep runs in the playoffs. The Avs at the time were loaded with world-class players such as Joe Sakic, Peter Forsberg, Milan Hejduk, Patrick Roy, and Chris Drury. Podein provided the grit on the third line and formed great chemistry with Stephane Yelle and Eric Messier. Once again, Podein laid his body on the altar of hockey.

Podein leans back on his stool in the ice rink lobby and curls up the inside of his lip to show me something.

"See how the inside of the lip hangs down low? That flap of skin is scar tissue," Podein says. "I was in Montreal and was taking a slap shot. I was falling to the ice and a guy slashed me right in the face, and I chipped my tooth and cut open the whole lip. Later on in the game, I fought the guy who did it, and he hit me again and busted it wide open a second time."

Podein pulls up the top lip a second time and exposes a tooth that is shorter than the others in the row. Then a crazed look comes into his eyes. The second part of the story comes to life, and he lets out a chuckle to himself. A cluster of children parades through the lobby, bags lugged over their shoulders as they trash-talk each other. Podein lets them pass by and then begins the story.

"Well, I'm in Colorado," Podein says. "My wife and I are fostering dogs. One of our foster dogs tries to kill my dog, so I run in to stop it. I've read that you're supposed to pull their tail and legs to get them off, and I do that, but nothing happened. Then I spray water. The foster dog still won't let go. So I go ahead and bite the dog in the neck. I bite as hard as I can, and I chip the same tooth again. The foster dog finally let go. I was so mad I ended up throwing the dog over a fence.

"I got the tooth fixed," Podein continues casually, as if a grown man biting a canine is an everyday event. "Then in Game Seven in the 2001 Stanley Cup Finals versus the Devils, I run into Devils defenseman Sean O'Donnell. It's a quick chip out and I'm going by him. Sean winds up and punches me right in the mouth and knocks the same tooth out again. I tell myself that I'm not going to get this tooth fixed anytime soon. I bust my lip, chip the tooth. I bite a dog and chip my tooth. Then I get the same one knocked out in Game Seven. Not bad."

The Avalanche won Game 7 and the Cup against the New Jersey Devils, and one of Podein's childhood dreams was achieved. Soaked in blood, sweat, tears, and beer inside the locker room after the win, Podein took a moment remember all the people who had helped him get there. He thought of Frank Serratore, the Rochester USHL coach who stuck his neck out and secured practice time for him with the UMD team that initially rejected him. He laughed about his days with Craig MacTavish, the longtime NHL veteran who mentored him and ensured the Flyers that Podein wouldn't be a problem if he joined the team. He thought of the 3M Line— him, Joel Otto, and Trent Klatt—and all their battles in the trenches together, three Minnesota boys playing on the same line in the NHL, and how sweet that was.

He looked around the locker room at current teammates like Joe Sakic and Peter Forsberg, two of the best players to ever play the game, who had helped him realize that because he was a mucker, his role on the team was invaluable. He thought of his wife and his parents and his brothers. He remembered all the kids he'd helped over the years when he volunteered. He remembered his '78 Vega and those long, snowy drives in the dead of a Minnesota winter with no heat and nothing but the bawdy old radio show *Sex Talk* to keep him company. He stood there in the Avalanche locker room soaked in memories—and a lot more and took it all in and wanted to stay in that moment for as long as he could.

So that's what he did. After Shjon Podein won the Stanley Cup, he stayed in his sweaty pads and jersey and skates for a full twenty-five hours after the game. He attended the post-game party in his pads and even danced on the dance floor in his skates. Note: This is not an NHL tradition.

Podein's son's practice session comes to a close under a barrage of whistles in the suburban Minneapolis hockey rink. Shjon helps his son get out of his pads, but then has to head to another anonymous ice rink with his teenage daughter for her hockey practice. More than likely, no one will ask him about his scars and the stories behind them. But that's okay with Podein. He knows he earned them the hard way, with honor and pride, and did it all for the team. He's just happy to be here in one piece, able to take his kids to practice and watch them play the game he loves. As a gesture for taking the time to talk,

I give Podein a six-pack of some local craft beer. His eyes light up, the scar tissue widens, and a chipped tooth is exposed, two small markings from his past life.

"I will give these six soldiers a good home in my belly," Podein says. When he opens the lobby doors, the summer sun greets his face while the frigid ice-rink air bids him farewell. He lets fly another giant smile, because life is good for the Mayor of Muckerville.

CHAPTER TWO
DAVE BROWN

In a different life, in a different version of the NHL, the man who stands before me in the press box at the Xcel Energy Center in St. Paul, Minnesota, possessed the ability to change the outcome of an entire hockey game with a single punch. You wouldn't know it by looking at him. With his standard corporate attire of suit, tie, and briefcase, this man could pass for an executive at any company in the world. The average person would have no idea that this docile, unassuming man was at one point in time a wiry 6'5" hockey enforcer who possessed a left hand that was as hard as a shovel, and when this man fought, he could dig his opponent a hole and bury an entire season or career in it, not just the body.

Dave Brown, fifty-three, is currently the head professional scout for the Philadelphia Flyers, and he's here to scout tonight's game between the Minnesota Wild and the Los Angeles Kings. During his playing career, spanning more than seven hundred NHL games from 1982 to 1996, Brown gained a reputation as one of the fiercest fighters to ever play in the league. He wasn't just a puncher, though. He was the real thing when the hockey world was full of bad men with horrible and violent reputations.

What made Brown different from the legions of tough guys in the old-time hockey era was the fact that after all the rumors were set aside, when all the hyperbole of a player's goonish antics had run out of steam, after all the voluminous braggadocio was dialed down and it was time to go one-on-one, he was one of the few players who could stop all the theatrics dead and set things straight with a methodical and stoic reckoning. When he went to work on a guy and fought during a hockey game, Brown could shed light on the limits of an opponent's—and an entire team's—toughness.

This, of course, was a different time in the NHL, when fighting and the on-ice tangos that came with it were ingrained in the sport. While he was a dependable and dedicated fourth-line player, Brown's main role was to patrol the ice. When things got hairy and his teammates were threatened, it was his job to root out the trouble on the opposing bench, bring the hooligans out, and tune them up. His fights were not for glory or fame but were simply to let the opposition know that if they wanted to take liberties with one of his smaller and more skilled teammates, his left fist was waiting.

"Back in my day, the quickest way to send a message to another team was by breaking someone's nose or jaw," Brown says humbly, his brutal words remarkably void of any machismo.

During Brown's career in the NHL, every team he played against had at least one designated tough guy. And he seemingly fought every one of them, often in hyped showdowns, to thunderous applause. Today this sort of predetermined bout between two hockey heavyweights is a bloodstained relic of another NHL. In the new era, teams have cleaved off the roster spot that was once occupied by a player like Brown, whose sole role was to provide toughness and to intimidate, and protect his teammates by dropping the gloves. Fighting is down league-wide, and indeed is reaching record lows. All the statistics and analytics now tell team management that they are losing production by rostering a player who plays a singular role in limited minutes. Although fighting is still allowed in hockey, it is no longer an actual tactic, the blunt instrument of intimidation that was once wielded around the league.

The modern NHL now has rules designed to curb fighting, such as the instigator rule, which penalizes the player who starts a fight more than his opponent. But it wasn't always this easy to brush aside the fights and intimidation. In the old days, if a team wanted to survive, they couldn't just simply turn the other cheek or hide in their shell. Brown knows this firsthand, because he physically and mentally lived through the wars of the NHL on the front lines.

"You had to have toughness back in the day for your team to be comfortable. If you weren't tough enough, then your best players couldn't play the way they needed to play," Brown says.

Back in the old-time hockey days, brawls and bench clears and other back-alley strategies were commonplace. That has all changed. If a team wants to goon it up, then their opponent will simply weather the storm and beat them on the power play. The last six Stanley Cup winners have done so without having to roster a player who was a designated heavyweight in a strict fighting role, and have instead relied on players who can contribute offensively and defensively while occasionally answering the bell to fight. In the modern NHL, speed, skill, and skating are now the desired trio for all players, and that means there simply isn't any more room for players like Dave Brown.

So here stands Dave Brown, a former fighter who currently wields a briefcase full of charts. He wrecked countless faces in his previous life, and an entire city nearly burned down with vitriol toward him after he pummeled the Calgary Flames' toughest tough guy during the historic Battle of Alberta (more on this later). But the same man today scouts teams and assiduously collects the desired analytics of the modern NHL, the minutiae of things like offensive-zone puck possession time after a face-off win.

He steps up and introduces himself to the press-box attendant, who stands at a podium.

"Dave Brown, with the Philadelphia Flyers," he says softly.

The press-box attendant scans the night's seating chart for his name. Her index finger slowly floats down a long list of the names of journalists, NHL staff, and various media types who are attending that night's game.

"Here you are. Your seat is number 112."

"Thank you," Brown says kindly.

As he moves through the press box, his presence is both commanding and comfortable. Those who recognize him nod in respect, because once you're an NHL heavyweight champ, you're always the champ. He finds his seat in a somewhat vacant section of the press row. The lights are hushed and intimate, like a law library. It's quiet down here where Brown sits, because all the journalists (like me) and beat writers are sequestered at the opposite end of the press box, hunched over and yapping and pecking at their keyboards. He quietly unpacks his briefcase, lines up his notes, and plugs in his phone.

He looks down pensively at the ice before tonight's game between the Wild and Kings. The players are warming up, circling their end of the ice like deranged ants. The arena shakes with the gyrating boom-bap of pop music.

"When I played, if the other team knew you could handle them, then you had a little bit of advantage," Brown says. "If you could be a little bit tougher than the other team, I think that would give your team a mental edge."

The mental edge that Dave Brown provided as a player came down like a guillotine. But to understand how fighting and players like Dave Brown used to shape the game of hockey, you first have to understand the dark corners where it used to be played.

FROM THE INCEPTION OF the sport to the early 1990s, professional hockey leagues were filled with fighters, roguish men who would not have been out of place in the *Star Wars* bar. These scarred and ill-tempered players with twisted noses, missing teeth, hammer hands, and colorful nicknames like "KO Kocur" and "Battleship Bob" didn't back down from anyone. They had reputations, valid or not, built on their history of on-ice violence. Fighting and on-ice thuggery had been used as an actual strategy since the start, because the general theory was that if you couldn't beat a team in the alley, then you couldn't beat them on the ice.

In this old-time hockey era, the games were often played at a constant simmer, a low heat that was applied through hard hits, scrums, stick work, and the occasional cheap shot. Depending on the severity of the actions, the intensity of the rivalry, and certainly the wiring of the players involved, a hockey game could boil over quickly. Because of this smoldering violence, every North American professional hockey team needed an enforcer, a man stout of heart and hands, a player who was hockey strong in immeasurable ways, to put out those fires and keep things in order. Fighting and the threat of fighting were, ironically, used to maintain peace on the ice. A player like Dave Brown was primarily employed as a deterrent: step out of line and see what happens.

Hockey is unique in the sense that the players policed their own game for decades with an unwritten honor system of what was considered to be acceptable behavior and what was over the line. If a player stepped outside this ancient honor system, the opposition could legally settle things and answer the infraction right there on the field of play.

For example, if an opponent slashed your star player or bumped your goalie, or if a tough guy on the other team took a cheap shot at a smaller and more skilled player, then that tough guy violated hockey's honor system and had to answer for his behavior. That retaliation usually came in the form of dropping the gloves and fighting. Teams that never answered the bell or never stood up to on-ice challenges were thought to be soft in the belly and, more important, in the hockey heart ,and were often trampled into submission.

Hockey has always had fighters and heated regional and divisional rivalries with spurts of berserker mayhem. But the crunch of fist-to-face gamesmanship became a permanent part of the NHL when the Philadelphia Flyers won back-to-back Stanley Cups in the 1970s with a team nicknamed the Broad Street Bullies, which was basically a Mad Max biker gang on skates. Because of the Flyers' success, which was largely engineered through their unrelenting on-ice pugilism—they were known for line brawls and bench clears and stick maiming and eye gouging—every team soon needed to protect itself. Hockey teams everywhere had to roster a few tough guys who were there to provide a stiff backbone, to not back down, to fight, and to intimidate.

This was the hockey world Dave Brown came up in. In 1981 he was just a teenager from Saskatoon, Saskatchewan, and admittedly not the best skater or stick handler. But he was hockey strong and a fearless kid in a big man's game, and, most important, he possessed that devastatingly long reach that could deliver the straight truth.

From an early age, Brown's left hand grabbed the attention of the hockey world. In traditional hockey fights where both combatants are right-handed, the fighters grab their opponent's jersey with their left hand and throw punches with their right. Since Dave Brown was left-handed, it threw everything off. His opponents had a hard time tying down his left fist, because the second the fight started he was already at work digging the hole he was going to put them in with a series of punches they couldn't stop. Worse still, he hit just as hard as Joe Kocur, the one-punch-knockout king in Detroit. By throwing left-handed, Brown could often tag men without impediment. In doing this, though, it exposed him to his opponent's right fist. But Brown stood in there and took punches as good as anyone in the league.

During the 1981–82 season with the Saskatoon Blades of the Western Hockey League (WHL), Brown was a mere nineteen years old and had 344 penalty minutes in just 62 games. During the next season, Brown eclipsed that with a staggering and record-breaking 418 penalty minutes in 71 games with the Maine Mariners of the AHL. The Mariners made the playoffs that year, too, and Brown tacked on an additional 107 penalty minutes. Plus, he got called up to the NHL that same year with the Philadelphia Flyers (in his first game in the NHL, Brown fought Boston Bruins tough guy Gord Kluzak and sent him to the hospital with a broken face) and added a few more penalty minutes, for a whopping grand total of 530 penalty minutes in a single season.

To put that total into perspective, an average penalty in the NHL is only two minutes. This is for slashing, interference, roughing, and all other garden-variety infractions. More serious penalties, such as fighting or misconduct, are still only five to ten minutes. An NHL player today who fights a lot and is known for rough play will average around 100 penalty minutes per season. So, for Brown to obtain more than 500 penalty minutes in a single season is an insane testament to his hockey strength and his uncompromising willingness to battle for his teammates. Whether it was a one-on-one bout or fighting an entire team, Brown was all in.

"Back in our day, in that time, it wasn't unusual to have a bench-clearing brawl," Brown says humbly, not mentioning at all the fact that he was involved in a bench-clearing brawl that rewrote the NHL rule book.

More than anything, though, it was Brown's job to make his teammates feel safe out on the ice. Brown was there to make sure the hard men and ogres on the other bench remained leashed and did not go after his team's young, skilled players; in that role, his sacrifice for his teammates was limitless.

Rick Tocchet is a former teammate of Brown's in Philadelphia and had a front-row seat.

"Dave Brown was the toughest player I ever played with," Tocchet says to me in a phone conversation. "He made us all look bigger than we were.

"Let me tell you a story about what Dave Brown meant to us," Tocchet continues excitedly. "When I was in juniors, all I heard about was this guy named Tim Coulis. The guy was crazy. The stories always got exaggerated. As the years went by, the stories got bigger."

As Tocchet battled his way up through the minor leagues of Canadian hockey, Tim Coulis's name haunted him. This was because during the mid to late 1980s, Coulis was the boogeyman, a real-life hockey brawler with a reputation shrouded in menace due to his many acts of on-ice violence. Tocchet played for the Sault Ste. Marie Greyhounds in the Ontario Hockey League (OHL), and at every turn, in every city, in every locker room, someone had a new story about Coulis that was worse than the previous one.

"Coulis didn't just beat up one guy, he beat up ten. Coulis didn't just break a guy's nose, he broke necks and jaws and ended guys' careers," Tocchet says. "Coulis didn't just fight a guy; he repeatedly and viciously punched him in the balls from close range. And did you hear the one about the time Coulis swung his stick at another player and almost maimed him for life?"

While Coulis was a decent, hard-nosed player, the stories about him were often exaggerated, the *Slap Shot*–style antics becoming established urban legend. But all fables start with a shred of truth. A lot of the stories that surrounded Coulis were based on real events, such as the time in 1982 when he punched out a referee. At the time of that incident, Coulis was twenty-four years old and playing for the Dallas Black Hawks in the Central League. After a penalty called on Coulis resulted in a power-play goal for the Salt Lake Golden Eagles, an enraged Coulis exited the penalty box and instantly went after referee Bob Hall, who had called the penalty on him.

Coulis menacingly skated circles around Hall in what was described as "an Indian and covered-wagon routine." Hall informed Coulis that if he didn't stop, he was going to receive a ten-minute misconduct. Coulis didn't stop, and Hall went back over to the penalty box and informed the other officials that Coulis was receiving the additional penalty. As Hall was informing the other players of the situation, Coulis popped Hall in the back of the head and knocked him out cold. Hall fell to the ice and had to be revived with ammonia.

At first Hall thought someone had thrown a bottle at him from the stands. (Hey, it was old-time hockey in the old Central League, a rough arena, and anything was possible.) Coulis was suspended for the rest of the season and kept away from the media for fear that he'd say something he and the team and the league would regret. But when Coulis stepped away from the game for a season, it only deepened the dark shadows that surrounded him.

Then, as fate would have it, Rick Tocchet and Tim Coulis crossed paths, and for the first time Tocchet came face-to-face with the specter who had haunted him for years.

"It was my first year with the Philadelphia Flyers," Tocchet says. "I was a rookie, and it was my first exhibition game. We were playing Minnesota, and Coulis was on a tryout with the North Stars. I'm eighteen years old and stretching at the blue line during warm-ups. And there's Tim Coulis. He's got no teeth and he looks like Freddy Krueger, and I'm shitting my pants."

As the teams warmed up, Tim Coulis had set his eyes on Tocchet, because Tocchet had garnered a solid reputation for himself as a fighter and a young, aggressive upstart, a player who possessed a unique blend of bare-knuckled moxie and scoring touch. Because of this, Tocchet knew that he was potentially a target, the type of person Coulis would challenge and try to intimidate and make a statement with.

But sitting next to Tocchet on the Flyer bench was Brown, a legitimate NHL tough guy with a cracking left fist. Tocchet leaned forward on the bench in the old Met Center in Bloomington, Minnesota, and saw with wide eyes that Dave Brown was no mere mortal NHL fighter. Dave Brown was a monster slayer.

"For me, it was like when you're a kid and there's the boogeyman, the Freddy Krueger. Well, on that night Dave Brown killed Freddy Krueger," Tocchet says, still in awe. "On Dave Brown's first shift he grabbed Tim Coulis and he just beat the living crap out of him. He broke Coulis's entire face."

Brown broke Coulis's orbital bone, crushing his face into pieces. In that one shift, in that one fight, Brown exemplified hockey strong, because he stepped up, set aside his own personal safety, and fought the bad guy so that his teammates didn't have to live in fear. Because of Brown's extinguishing of Tim Coulis, Tocchet was finally unshackled of the fear that had haunted him for years in the minor leagues. So, naturally, on Tocchet's next shift he played like a free man.

"I went out onto the ice and ran every guy I could," Tocchet says, his hearty guffaw rattling the phone speaker. "I hit four Minnesota players in a row straight from behind, because when you have the guy who broke the orbital bone of the boogeyman on your side, you can get away with anything!"

Tim Coulis was soon cut from the North Stars and he never made it in the NHL. Although Coulis's toughness was without question, his antics and his legend lasted slightly longer than his career of about nineteen games with the Washington Capitals. Meanwhile, Dave Brown played in 729 games over fourteen seasons in the NHL, earning 1,789 penalty minutes, and his reputation as one of the most feared and respected tough guys to ever play the game has been permanently stamped in the annals.

But physical strength and a hard chin can take a hockey fighter only so far. Brown and all the other enforcers had to possess not only an untold amount of physical strength but also mental toughness. As a team's designated tough guy, there was always someone on the opposing team, in the next game, in the next town, preparing to destroy them, and looking to make a reputation by kicking their ass. And if they didn't fight or got beaten too often, they could lose their job and be thrown onto the NHL scrap heap like so many disposable tough guys before them. After all, a general manager could always find someone else who was willing to step in and fight.

Courage is in all hockey players, in various forms: playing in pain is in the very fabric of the game. But the hockey strength and courage it takes to be a fighter is something else entirely. Fighters like Brown had to live with the fear of being beaten, of being humiliated, and of being savagely injured. That fear was a living thing. No matter how far a player pushed his fears of being beaten to the corners of his mind, brushing the mental anguish and physical pain to the side and summoning the courage to stand in there and fight again, there were always crumbs of that anxiety left behind. The fear never left them; there was another game in two days and another tough guy to potentially deal with, and that tough guy could hurt you so bad you just might not ever recover. This was what Dave Brown and countless other players like him lived through day after day, season after season. From the broken bones in their faces to the scars on their hands to the concussive waves that rippled through their brains, their sacrifice to the team was paid in full.

But, in typical Brown fashion, he downplays his sacrifice, his toughness, and the pop-culture glorification of his role.

"I mean, I've been cut a bunch of times and went back into the game. But that's nothing," Brown says casually. "Besides a bloody nose and a cut here and there and a few breaks, I survived just fine."

Brown pauses for a quick second to reflect on his sacrifice. He sets down his pen and then crosses his arms. He is suited and scholarly looking. But underneath the fine tweed and polished shoes, he's still got the rough-hewn charm of Indiana Jones as a professor. Look closely past all of it and you'll see the nicks and scars from his adventurous playing career; they give him a ruggedness that can't entirely be polished away.

"Jeez, I never lost any teeth. They've been loosened a little bit, but nothing major," Brown continues. "I cracked my foot, broke bones in my hands, and broke a few ribs. But I avoided the catastrophic injuries that were a routine part of the job for players in my role. There were a lot more guys that were a lot more beat up than me because they played a lot more minutes than me. I'm not nearly as bad as a lot of guys are physically."

Despite the obvious hazards to his mind and body, Brown showed up every day at the rink for his teammates. His reputation was built slowly and steadily, one game after another, one shift after another, and eventually, one fight after the next. He would suit up, climb over the boards, and engage. That was his job. When he fought, it was a laborious affair, no different than a man digging a ditch.

"I took as many as I got," Brown says humbly. "Everybody asks me who the toughest guy I fought was. Back in my day, everyone had a tough guy, and he was someone to deal with, and it wasn't easy. What people don't realize is that everyone was tough. If you had a bad night, you could get beat by any-body. I found it as difficult as anyone else fighting me. It was tough for me to fight everyone."

HUMILITY ASIDE, DAVE BROWN was so effective at his job and struck such fear in other players that teams had to strate-gize ways to neutralize him, which is an amazing fact consider-ing he was a fourth-line guy who played limited minutes. His time on the Edmonton Oilers, when he was a foot soldier on the front lines in the Battle of Alberta—a provincial grudge match between the Calgary Flames and the Edmonton Oilers that took place in the late 1980s and early '90s—was a prime example of what he could provide a team.

"The rivalry was intense for a long time, probably as intense as any rivalry in the history of the league," Brown points out. "Calgary just happened to be in the same division and confer-ence as Edmonton. If they were on the other side, they probably would have gone to the finals as much as the Oilers."

Between 1983 and 1990, the Edmonton Oilers and the Calgary Flames represented the Western Conference in the Stanley Cup Finals a combined eight times (Edmonton won five Cups and lost one, while Calgary won one and lost one). But the Battle of Alberta was more than just a pumped-up sports rivalry. Their hate was personal, a bristling animos-ity between two towns in the same province that dated back centuries.

During the 1980s, the malice between Edmonton, the capital and more liberal city, and Calgary, the western cowboy and oil town with a more conservative bent, manifested itself in the form of two elite hockey teams that were conveniently in the same conference. This created an arms race of talent through the 1980s and '90s, with both teams stockpiling elite talent as well as grinders of the dirtiest ilk. Edmonton had a quiver loaded with Wayne Gretzky, Mark Messier, Jari Kurri, Paul Coffey, Glenn Anderson, and Grant Fuhr. Calgary countered with Joe Nieuwendyk, Joe Mullen, Doug Gilmour, Al MacInnis, Lanny McDonald, Gary Roberts, and Mike Vernon. But the Flames also had Joel Otto and Tim Hunter, and they were there to make life miserable for the talented Oiler players. The Oilers countered with Marty McSorley, Don Jackson, Dave Semenko, and, of course, Dave Brown.

In a much-anticipated home-and-home pair of games between Calgary and Edmonton in January 1990, the Calgary Flames called up a player named Stu Grimson from the minor leagues to counterbalance Brown. Grimson, 6'6" and 240 pounds, was a tough young stud playing for the Salt Lake Golden Eagles in the IHL who had amassed more than 300 penalty minutes and was reportedly undefeated in fights. In the first game between Calgary and Edmonton, Grimson and Brown fought twice. Grimson got some solid shots in, and when a previous cut reopened on Brown, a good amount of blood spewed.

"In that that series, Stu Grimson made his name," says Paul Ranheim, a former Calgary Flames forward. "I will never forget that first night in Edmonton. Stu caught Brown off his game, and Brown was pissed. It all ended up in the papers, too. A tale of the tape. It was all building, and we knew it was going to be a battle the next game."

Calgary ended up winning the Edmonton game 3–1. In the postgame interviews, Grimson and the Calgary staff and a few other players had some choice things to say. The media stoked the fire between the two men—and, more important, the two teams—by declaring that Grimson had won the fights and handled himself against the heavyweight Brown.

Two days later, the teams played again in the Saddledome in Calgary. In the opening minutes of the second game, Brown went to work to set things straight, to do the job he had to do, and this time he was going to do it correctly.

Four minutes into the first period, Brown and Grimson dropped the gloves, and Brown delivered a beating so absolute that it still stands as one of the worst ever in the NHL. Brown unleashed a torrent of lefts that instantly buckled Grimson. Brown hit Grimson with so much conviction it was like a stern reckoning not just between two players but between two teams and two cities. Grimson took the punches with barely any defense and was lunging and grasping desperately for a grip, like a man falling through a hole in the ice. As the two men spun around, Brown kept lashing his left fist into Grimson's face, savagely breaking his cheek and orbital bone.

"I was sitting on the bench ten feet away," Ranheim says gravely. "They're dancing, and Brown catches Stu and you could hear this *pop*. It was frightening."

Brown knocked Grimson to the ice in a flailing heap and then fell on top of him. When the fight was over, Brown rose to one knee on the ice and for a second simply inspected his left hand for damage. Then Brown got up slowly and stood menacingly before everyone. He did not strut. He did not puff up. He did not point. He just turned his cold, angry eyes toward the entire Calgary bench and gave them a piercing look.

Grimson headed to the penalty box and served his full five-minute penalty with his face completely broken. It was the worst beating of his career.

"He broke my cheekbone and fractured my orbital bone in three places," Grimson says. "I had to have reconstructive surgery to square it all away."

After he served his penalty, Grimson skated across the ice and instantly retreated to the locker room and removed his pads. Then he headed straight to the hospital. The Oilers went on to win the Stanley Cup that year.

"That moment, that fight, might have been the end for a lot of guys," says Ranheim. "But Stu was mentally tough. He knew what he wanted. He knew what he could do, and he wasn't afraid."

The very next season the Battle of Alberta raged on. The Flames finished above the Oilers during the regular season, and the two teams met in the 1991 playoffs. With the Oilers up two games to one in the series, the Flames were looking for a spark. In the third period of Game 4, with Edmonton leading 5–2, the Flames' main fighter, Tim Hunter, a rugged man with a legendary hockey schnoz that was pounded steeper than a black-diamond ski slope, jumped a face-off. Hunter proceeded to have words with the Oilers' Steve Smith and stuck him with his stick; a scrum ensued. Brown was naturally on the ice as the counterweight to Hunter and moved in to mediate. Then the Flames' Gary Roberts face-washed Smith, and the fuse was lit.

Flames defenseman Jim Kyte, strong as a bull, paired up with Brown, and they ended up fighting. After trading blows for a few seconds, Brown knocked Kyte to the ice. Brown's punches had carried him forward, and he leaned over the fallen Flame. As Brown crouched there, he held back his punches, because Kyte was clearly vulnerable. During this unilateral cease-fire, Kyte unwisely used the opportunity to sneak in a few punches. He tagged Brown in the face.

This incensed Brown.

Joel Otto, the ursine Calgary centerman, was right there during the Brown beatdown of Kyte. Years later in Philadelphia, when Otto was a teammate of both Shjon Podein and Dave Brown, he regaled Podes with the story.

"Brownie's got Kyte on the ground. Brown's right arm of his jersey was always loose. He was a pure lefty, and the left sleeve was so tight you couldn't even snap it. It had been shortened all the way up to the elbow pad, too," Podein says. "[Now]

Brown's on top of Kyte and pounding him. As he pounded him he asked him, 'Do you give up? Do you give up?' Kyte said, 'Hell no!'"

Brown pounded Kyte mercilessly right into the ice, to the point where his own Edmonton teammates tried to step in and stop him.

Minutes after destroying Kyte, though, Brown helped the man he had just beaten into submission get up from the ice. As they skated around, clutched together, it appeared that Brown was holding Kyte up. For several minutes Brown talked to a wobbling Kyte as the latter stared glassy-eyed around the arena. Concussed, with noodles for legs, having just been buried alive and resurrected, Kyte was like the skating dead.

"Kyte goes to the locker room and looks Joel Otto in the face and says, 'Joel, don't say anything. I've been beat up a lot worse than this,'" Podein says, laughing hysterically. "Dave Brown was scary tough."

It is now the third period between the Wild and Kings, and the game has gone on without incident: no fights, light checking, and just a few minor scrums. The Wild are a light team that relies on speed and transitions to win games, while the Kings deploy a heavy and mobile unit that prefers to lean on their opponents and wear them down. These two conflicting styles generate little real friction and heat. While the skill and speed on the ice tonight are world-class, the physical engagement between the teams is like a pillow fight compared to the action Brown used to see, particularly on one historic night in Montreal in 1987.

"That was just something that just came to a head," he says calmly.

The "that" which he mentions is a legendary bench-clearing brawl, and one of the worst black eyes in NHL history. It occurred on May 14, 1987, at the Montreal Forum in Game 6 of the Prince of Wales Conference Finals between the Montreal Canadiens and the Philadelphia Flyers.

Young Montreal agitator Claude Lemieux, a classic needling villain with a grating playing style, had a ritual of shooting a puck into the opposing team's net after warm-ups were over. The Flyers, a surly team guided by fiery and irritable coach Mike Keenan, were sick of Lemieux's ritual (and certainly sick of his antics). So Lemieux was warned by multiple Flyers not to do it or else something was going to happen.

"They had that superstition thing where Lemieux and Shayne Corson put the puck in our net," Brown explains. "Flyer Ed Hospodar said we were going to put a stop to it. And it grew out of that."

The Canadiens and the Flyers cleared the ice after warm-ups. Sure enough, though, Lemieux snuck back onto the ice with Montreal's Shayne Corson to complete their ritual of shooting the puck into the Flyers' now-empty net. Ed Hospodar and Flyers goalie Chico Resch were waiting in the wings, and when they saw Lemieux sneak back onto the ice, they rushed out to stop him.

As the Forum organist tapped out a lovely swaying song, with dozens of pucks still littering the ice from warm-ups and the referees and NHL officials in their locker room, the entire Philadelphia Flyers team poured out of the tunnel, and soon the ice was filled with players. It was a classic bench-clearing brawl, if by benches you mean the ones in the locker rooms. The game hadn't even started yet.

"You don't expect something like that to happen in the pregame of a playoff game," Brown says laughing.

The Flyers and Canadiens fought in giant rolling waves across the ice. There were no referees, no league officials, no one in sight to stop it. The stands were sparsely populated, and the fans looked on like observers at a zoo. Some of the Flyers were only half-dressed in their undershirts and elbow pads. Some were still in shower sandals. Flyers coach Keenan had dressed more players for the warm-up than normal, and the Flyers now outnumbered the Canadiens by several players. The then-young Montreal goalie Patrick Roy came onto the ice like a shining white knight in his crisp Canadiens home jersey and white leg pads and tried to intervene.

"I went out onto the ice, and I knew I was going to fight Chris Nilan," Brown says, referring to the renowned Montreal tough guy. "Nilan was my matchup. So I went looking for him."

Brown and Nilan were drawn together as if by magnetic force. On one side of the mass of players was Nilan, who looked annoyed as he weaved his way through the throng of players. On the other end of the ice was Brown, bare-chested in his elbow pads and suspenders, skating across the ice toward him. In the middle of the angry ocean of players they finally and inevitably came together, and the main attraction was under way. Well, except for the fact that Nilan had nothing to hold on to, because Brown didn't have his jersey on. Nilan was also outsized by five inches and so he smartly retreated, skating backward, trying to come up with a strategy to handle the bare-skinned Brown, who kept pressing forward and was rapidly closing the gap between them.

Nilan grabbed the back of Brown's suspenders and got in close, face to chest. Punches were thrown four and five at a time. Then they would rest. Then four more punches. Then they'd rest some more. Brown got Nilan down to the ice, and then they got back up. Brown was looking to hold Nilan out and away from him so he could drop long-range bombs on him. But Nilan, as always, stayed in close and tight and buried his head in Brown's bare chest, keeping his punches short.

"At one point, we were kind of catching our breath," Nilan says. "Brown asked, 'You had enough?' I threw another punch at him, and away we went again. It went forever."

The referees eventually appeared, and after thirty minutes everything leveled off, and one of the worst pregame brawls in hockey history came to an end. As players left the ice, the organist played on. But just to make sure that no more lines were crossed, no more shenanigans stirred up, Brown circled the ice near his bench, the last workingman left at the job site, mopping things up.

A few Montreal players loitered around as Brown prowled back and forth, his suspenders ripped apart, welts all over his back, his hair a large salad, his pads in disarray. When he finally exited the ice, the Montreal fans hanging over the railing greeted him with a round of boos and vinegary taunts. Brown reached the tunnel and a small smile peeked out, because even he knew that the league was going to have a field day with what had gone on. And the NHL did: Rule 71, enacted the next season, prohibited players from leaving the bench to fight, limited the number of players allowed in pregame warm-ups, and introduced big fines for coaches or management who lost control of their players. The era of the bench clear and large-scale brawling came to an end, largely due to Brown's near-twenty-minute shirtless fight with Nilan.

BROWN WILL ALWAYS DOWNPLAY his status as one of hockey's toughest players, as one of the game's greatest fighters, regardless of what is said about him. That is just his nature.

Besides a fifteen-game suspension he received for cross-checking Tomas Sandstrom in the head in 1987, which was retaliation for a vicious spear to the groin that Sandstrom uncorked on the Flyers' world-class defenseman Mark Howe,

Brown's long and bruising career was largely devoid of the antics and dark theatrics that surrounded the brawlers of his time. After he fought he didn't show the roaring crowds a bunch of flamboyant hand jives. He wasn't going to humiliate another fighter like that. He wasn't going to showboat. Brown wasn't a part of a legendary duo, either, a heavyweight tag team of hockey fighters like Bob Probert and Joe Kocur. And he certainly wasn't out there running through the night, tearing up the city, and playing up the role of the antihero that some NHL tough guys were known for. He was married to a high school math teacher.

Brown simply had a shovel for a left fist, and he diligently went to work and sacrificed everything because he was serving a higher purpose: he was protecting his teammates so that they could go out and not be hurt or scared; they would have the freedom to do their job and, ultimately, have successful careers.

"I had an obligation to the people sitting in the dressing room," Brown says. "If I wasn't doing my job, I felt like I had let the team down, and that was more disappointing than taking a punch to the mouth."

Tonight's game between the Wild and the Kings ends. The arena rock fades and transitions into exit music. Dave Brown quietly packs up his things and unassumingly walks down a now-empty press row back toward the elevator that will take him out of the arena. Because of the nature of his job, there will soon be another elevator in another arena and another press box in another city. You would never know by looking at him, but at one point in time, in a previous life, in a different era, this man with the suit and tie and briefcase was one of the most feared men in all of hockey. This astute and docile hockey scout fought the worst men his sport had to offer, and he buried them, one at a time, in an NHL boneyard.

CHAPTER THREE
THE GRIND LINE

In the 1994–95 Stanley Cup Finals, the Detroit Red Wings, a bullet train of a hockey team with 70 points in 48 games and arguably the most talented bunch of players in the league, faced off against the utilitarian New Jersey Devils, a John Deere tractor in their solid mechanics, steady performance, and reliability. This is not to say the 1995 Devils were a bunch of no-talent rubes, though. The Devils were workers. They were a balanced team, nothing too high and nothing too low. But instead of blowing by every opponent at a breakneck speed, as the Red Wings did, the Devils won a majority of their games with a steady, assembly-line mentality.

When the 1995 finals started the overwhelming consensus was that Detroit would beat the Devils; the belief was based solely on the Red Wings' astonishing talent level. But games aren't won by blabbering media wonks. Games are won on the ice, and in playoff games in particular, games are won in the slop in front of the net, behind the plow along the boards, and in the hard ground in the corners. In four games, Detroit coach Scotty Bowman, the winningest coach in NHL history and a man who won thirteen Stanley Cups as a player, coach, or manager, saw the sweep go the other way as the Devils won their first Stanley Cup in franchise history, ending the series with a humiliating, brooms-out beatdown in Game 4.

During the series, Bowman and the Red Wings saw many things: the Devils turning the ice into a swamp, slowing the skilled Detroit forwards to a crawl; a young Devils goalie named Martin Brodeur finding his playoff legs; a gritty team with muscle and size and goals from all four lines; and Devils coach Jacques Lemaire winning with less in a deliberate, numbing shutdown strategy in the neutral zone.

There was a largely unheralded factor, though, to New Jersey's dominance. It was big and surly and belligerent, and it would ironically inspire the Red Wings' future turnaround. It was the Devils' fourth line of Randy McKay, Mike Peluso, and Bobby Holik, which ran over the Red Wings and changed the momentum of entire periods and games. In the end the line played a massive role in the humbling sweep of the more talented Wings.

The Devils' fourth line was famously nicknamed the Crash Line, because its playing style was like a snub-nose Peterbilt semitruck without brakes. Separately, each player was slightly above average and had his own unique talents, but they were nothing you wouldn't find on other teams: McKay was a hard-nosed winger with a decent scoring touch; Peluso was a wild man, a lanky and long-haired tough guy whose fighting strategy consisted of swinging as hard as he could as many times as he could until he fell down, hoping to land at least a few punches; and Holik was a minotaur of a centerman, part bull, part man. When Devils coach Jacques Lemaire put the three players together, though, they were considered to be the best fourth line in the league.

The Crash Line was so heavy and abrasive that they changed the flow of the game with their hits and aggression and timely goals (in the 1995 Cup playoffs alone, McKay had two goals in the Boston series and Holik had two in the Pittsburgh series; they both chipped in points in the finals; and Peluso did his pillaging Viking routine and hit everything in sight), and they were especially effective in the playoffs, when every inch of the ice was precious real estate.

"We were momentum keepers or momentum changers," McKay says. "We could hit and score a few goals here and there through a campaign, through the playoffs. We were put on the ice after every goal scored for or against. It was to either keep momentum going or to get some momentum built."

The Red Wings had the talent to win it all, with danglers and snipers and Hall of Famers aplenty. But it wasn't always about the big-name players, the stars whom everyone knows and wants, the shiny free-agent pieces added and subtracted every season. A Stanley Cup–winning team also needs to have the dark matter that surrounds those stars and blinding lights, the binding agents that tie it all together and give it shape.

But building a hockey team is tricky, a science unto itself. The word *chemistry* is thrown around a lot in the sports world. Fans and reporters alike love to talk about the symbiotic relationship between teammates and how they form an instinctual and near-magical bond in their scoring and passing and positioning the field of play and in their relationships in the locker room.

In hockey, chemistry can be seen in a variety of ways, but it's primarily in the line combinations of the three forwards, defensive pairings, power-play units, and penalty-kill tandems. Chemistry can be formed between teammates, like Wayne Gretzky and Jari Kurri, over years of repetition and playing together, or it can be created when complementary players instantly gel, like the legendary defensive pairing of Nicklas Lidstrom and Brian Rafalski. Coaches are constantly tinkering with player combinations to try to blend different attributes—a crafty passer with a shooter, a defenseman who likes to rush the puck forward and attack with a stay-at-home defenseman who minds the fort—in an attempt to form units that are fluid and cohesive and contribute to the offensive and defensive game plan.

The goal-scoring and point-producing chemistry of the skilled forwards and shutdown defensemen are what produce media coverage. The chemistry used to form the bottom lines, though, the third- and fourth-line combinations of the grinders and irritants like the Crash Line, is the dirty science of hockey, the sort of rogue experimenting that would make

Walter White proud. It is in this underground laboratory, the one where the intangible elements are mixed together, that success is often born. Teams that survive the marathon of the regular season and the slog of the playoffs do so by having a deep roster, and that means having quality third and fourth lines that can play big minutes in the muck, chip in goals, and change the tide of a game with hits and the sort of tire-iron hockey that leaves a mark.

After being plowed under by the Devils, and particularly the Crash Line, Detroit later assembled what would become known as the Grind Line, the infamous combination of Kris Draper, Kirk Maltby, and Joe Kocur (and later Darren McCarty), a forward line of three players with volatile on-ice personalities that the Wings hoped could combat the behemoths of the Eastern Conference, like New Jersey, Boston, and Philadelphia.

The chemistry of Detroit's Grind Line was nearly instant. Each one of the players had been cast aside at some point by another team. They were random parts, undervalued in other organizations or exiled in a sort of semiretirement, and they finally found the right fit with each other, their different playing styles blending together like a witch's brew: Maltby was a swift skater and goal-scoring machine turned checker, whose on-ice personality was as pleasant as a screaming can of tear gas; he was acquired as an afterthought in a trade-deadline deal with Edmonton. Kocur was pulled out of a beer league hockey team that the Detroit Red Wings describe on their website as an "Industrial Hockey League," after his decade-long career as one of the most feared fighters in the 1980s had ended. Draper was traded to Detroit by the Winnipeg Jets for future consideration (which was literally one dollar) and was a flame-bearded Chuck Norris on skates, a smack-talking firebrand and speedster. Darren McCarty was added after Kocur's retirement, a bushwhacking frontiersman who wielded knuckles and a nice scoring touch. When the players were mixed together, the result was highly flammable; it would eventually become the greatest fourth line in the history of the game because of its winning, longevity, and, above all, its relentless pugnaciousness.

"I think the toughest part of playing against us back in the day was that we all brought different things," Draper says. "McCarty was a tough guy who loved to fight. But he also scored a hat trick in the 2002 conference finals versus Colorado. Maltby was a really strong skater and loved to hit. Shake Kocur's hand, see his hand. He's had over twenty-two surgeries or something like that, and it's an old beaten-down leather football [from fighting]. We could all skate and finish checks and score big goals."

SHJON PODEIN BATTLED THE Grind Line when he played for the Philadelphia Flyers, who were swept by the Red Wings in the Stanley Cup Finals (more on that later), and when he went head-to-head with them in the bloody Avalanche–Red

Wings rivalry (a lot more on that later). "But we had a different name for them. We called them the PITA Line. As in 'Pain In The Ass.'"

"I take that as a compliment," Kris Draper says, laughing. "I think if another team or organization thinks I was a pain in the ass to play against, I was doing something right. That's a compliment to the three of us."

The Grind Line was formed after the Red Wings were swept in the 1995 Stanley Cup Finals by the Devils, and, as mentioned earlier, it helped lead to a Detroit turnaround. The Red Wings returned to the Cup finals two years later with the Grind Line intact and swept the Philadelphia Flyers to end the Red Wings' forty-two-year Cup drought. What separates the Grind Line from other fourth lines in hockey history is the fact that they not only epitomized every single aspect of the hockey-strong ethos—a blue-collar outfit of skill and belligerence that played in pain, battled back from adversity, fought and hit, stuck up for their teammates, and scored huge goals—but they won a lot (ahem, four Cups).

The four primary members of the Grind Line—Kris Draper, Kirk Maltby, Joe Kocur, and Darren McCarty—played more than three thousand games combined, and each has had numerous moments of glory and gore. Their true greatness can be seen in four single moments in their long careers that together give us the true meaning of hockey strong.

Kris Draper

Kris Draper did not see the hit that would obliterate the right side of his face coming. It was Game 6 of the 1996 Western Conference Finals between the Red Wings and the Colorado Avalanche, and Draper was hit from behind at full throttle by Avalanche forward Claude Lemieux; it drove him face-first into the side boards with a sickening thud. The blow broke Draper's nose, jaw, cheek, and orbital bone, caved in an entire row of teeth, and produced facial lacerations that took forty stitches on the inside and outside of his face to close. But the damage didn't stop at the surface. When Lemieux smashed Draper's face into the side boards—the collision resembles a crash test dummy being rammed into a partition—Draper's brain suffered a major concussion. Seconds after impact the Red Wings' trainer hopped over the boards and covered Draper's face with a towel, for it was already in ruins. The towel instantly filled with blood.

Moments later, Kris Draper lay on the training table in the Red Wings' locker room. When Draper wiggled his way out of the concussive fuzz in his head—he had been slipping in and out of consciousness—the first thing he did was not to call out in pain or moan for sympathy—instead he started putting his pads back on: Draper still wanted to play. Despite the multiple broken bones and the monstrously swollen face, despite all the wreckage in his mouth, despite slipping in and out of consciousness, despite the blood pouring out of his face, despite the fact that he could see out of only one eye . . . despite all of it, Kris Draper's first instinct was to try to get back into the game.

"Where do you think you're going?" the NHL doctor asked Draper when he noticed him reaching for his gear. After all, here was an athlete in no condition to eat a cracker, let alone compete in a professional sporting event.

"I'm going back to finish the game," Draper told the doctor through his badly broken jaw as he reached over and started pulling on his gloves.

This all might sound like lunacy, that a man with a crushed face, unable to see, speak, eat, breath through his nose, or even think clearly would still want to carry on, all in the effort to play a game. But Kris Draper was a hockey player, and that is what hockey players do. They carry on. They play in pain. Sure, the injuries sucked. But not playing was worse. Despite the fact that his body had been broken and he had suffered a traumatic head injury, there was still something untouchable and unbreakable buried deep inside Kris Draper that was guiding him off that training table.

"Any time I had an injury," Draper says, "and they said I'd be back in two to four weeks, I tried to make sure it was two weeks or less. That was the mind-set. That was expected. You played hockey and you were going to get cut and you got back out there."

That's why Kris Draper wanted back in the game even when he was shattered to pieces. He was a part of all of it. He felt the history of the game tugging inside of him; he felt that thread that connected him to all the players who had worn the famous winged wheel on the front of the Detroit sweater and had battled back from injury. He owed it to his teammates and to the Detroit organization that had picked him up after the Winnipeg Jets dumped him. He owed it to the fans and to the city of Detroit, a no-nonsense kind of town that above all things appreciates an honest effort.

"I thought, Hey, man, just don't pass me the puck from my blind side and we'll go from there," Draper says, laughing. "Then they walked me over to the mirror and told me to take a look."

For the first time, he saw his massively swollen and bloodied face, a face that would later require a three-hour surgery and his jaw to be wired shut for six weeks. His nose was crushed, and he couldn't breathe through it. The orbital bone was broken, too, but you couldn't tell, because the jaw and cheekbone had swollen so monstrously that they engulfed everything else. At that moment, the NHL doctor used some quintessential hockey understatement.

"They said I was done for the night," Draper says, aghast as he recalls the absurdity.

Done for the night. Even the doctor, a man of science with years of medical schooling and training, had to give credence to the fact that no matter the severity of a hockey player's injury, you could simply never count him out.

"It looked bad," Kirk Maltby says. "Once we got on the plane I remember seeing the whole side of his face and jaw area and cheek. It looked like someone had blown up his face with an air pump."

It was no mistake that Lemieux found Draper there along the side boards. While no player ever deserves to suffer such a horrific injury, Draper was a defensive centerman and made his living right there in the dirty areas of the rink, the areas of intense physical contact between the players along the side walls and in front of the net and in the corners. That is where Draper plied his trade, with all the fury of a rioter with a pitchfork and torch.

Draper paid a heavy price for all that time on the Grind Line battling against the top lines during the regular season and the playoffs. The physical toll of his defensive work compounded over the twenty years he spent in the NHL—more than one thousand games altogether.

"The ultimate compliment came from Scotty Bowman," Draper says. "He trusted us. He trusted the Grind Line in big situations. In the last minute of the game he trusted us to kill penalties. We played against all the top players, like Sakic, Forsberg, Modano, and Gretzky, and all the top lines. We took a lot of pride in that. I took all the face-offs. I always felt that if I could win the draw, then those skilled guys would have to work harder to get the puck back."

During his long career, Draper played against a lot of men who were bigger and stronger; now the history of the game and its mantra of playing in pain is inscribed on his body.

"Ask any NHL player who has played over one thousand games like I did, and they'll say the same thing. There's a lot of wear and tear on the body," Draper says humbly.

"Kris got cut so many times it seemed like if someone went by him fast, the wind would cut him," Maltby jokes. "It was never a nick. It was always three stitches here, five there. I don't recall a guy getting cut more times than Kris did. He'd get it done right away and come back or wait till after."

"I've had over two hundred stitches. Nothing major, though," Draper says. "I've broken my wrist, dislocated my thumb, separated both shoulders, played in the playoffs with broken ribs, and tweaked both my ACL and MCL. But it was a game I loved, and you find a way to keep playing."

In 1996, Draper's passion for the game was tested with that horrific facial injury.

"It was a tough summer," Draper admits in regard to both the physical and emotional pain he suffered.

"He had all the [jaw] surgeries afterward," Maltby says. "I saw him once or twice that summer, and he had to carry pliers around with him in case he got sick and had to cut the wires out."

Draper lost fifteen pounds and had to take all of his meals through a straw; meanwhile, Lemieux was suspended for only two games and ended up winning the Stanley Cup for the second year in a row (Lemieux was a member of the New Jersey Devils the year before, when they swept the Red Wings in the Cup finals).

"But the one thing I said back then was that the hit wasn't going to affect the way I played the game," Draper says proudly. "I was going to go out and play the only way I knew how, and that was hard and I was going to work my ass off."

During his time in rehab the ancient code of hockey strong was still very much alive inside him. Kris Draper may have been done for the night after his face was crushed, but his will was intact, and, in fact, stronger than ever before. In seventeen seasons with Detroit, Draper remarkably never missed the playoffs, playing in 220 playoff games and winning four Stanley Cups. He was a four-time member of Canada's world championship team and represented Team Canada in 2006 in the Olympics in Turin, Italy; in 2004 he won a Selke Award for Top Defensive Forward in the NHL.

To this day, you won't hear Draper cry about the hit that obliterated the right side of his face and caused permanent damage. The area is still numb. But Kris Draper shrugs it all off.

"The teeth are okay," Draper says. "That's important. They're still in there."

Joe Kocur

On October 16, 1986, a massive bronze statue weighing four tons was erected in Detroit's Hart Plaza. The statue, of a giant clenched right fist, was appropriately named *The Fist*. Created by world-renowned artist Robert Graham, the statue was twenty-four feet long and twenty-four feet high, and was suspended in the air by three steel beams that were propped in a tripod. *The Fist* floated in the air as if it were a punch being thrown; it honored Detroit native Joe Louis's power both in the boxing ring and in breaking down racial stereotypes.

I like to think that Graham's statue also doubles as a fist of steel that belonged to another famous citizen of the Motor City, a Red Wing forward named Joe Kocur. Kocur possessed a human fist, of course, not a piece of art. It was made of flesh and bone and something ungodly, and yet it, too, was unbreakable. It hit harder than nearly any fist before it, and because of this, it was a right hand that came with more warning labels than any other fist in the history of the league. It broke helmets, destroyed faces, and ended careers.

The first shot dismantled the hinges and loosened everything up. The second was absolute destruction, the kind of blow that takes a door down. If the Graham statue is a symbol of Joe Louis's strength both as an athlete and as a vehicle for societal change, for a better, brighter, more tolerant world, Kocur's right hand was the opposite: a symbol of annihilation, extinguishing all hope, bringing only darkness to those in its reach.

"Shaking his hand was like shaking a cement block," Maltby says, his disbelief clear. Kocur has had numerous surgeries on his hand, and the layers of scar tissue that have built up over his knuckles have rendered his fist a virtual war club.

"Most people, when they make a fist, the skin tightens up. His hand is one big piece of scar tissue from punching helmets and visors and faces. His right hand was known for throwing the hardest punches ever in fights," Maltby adds.

Draper also expresses amazement. All his years of watching Joe Kocur wreck faces with his right fist left him astonished by one fact.

"When you saw Bob Probert or Marty McSorley or Donald Brassard, you saw their size," Draper says. "The amazing thing is, as tough as Kocur was and how hard he punched, he was not a big guy."

Most NHL fighters during the 1980s and '90s had their own techniques: Bob Probert was all about endurance and would engage in drawn-out, jersey-tearing melees; Chris Nilan liked to get in close and tie down an opponent's arms and fire off short punches; Dave Brown was 6'5" and left-handed and wanted to do the opposite of Nilan—that is, he'd string his opponent out and away from him and tag him with long-range missiles targeted directly at their eye sockets or nose; and Craig Berube was a straight-out brawler. Joe Kocur had one plan, and it was to hit you with his right hand. Everyone knew it, too, but no one could stop it. All he needed to do was connect once with his right fist, and down came the wall.

Jim Kyte was a snarling 6'5", 210-pound defenseman for the Winnipeg Jets when he took on Kocur on November 25, 1988. In a split second, Kocur hit Kyte in the head with a single thunderous punch that buckled Kyte's entire body, his helmet instantly popping off. With all the walls and levels of protection now loosened up, Kocur shoved in the battering ram; this one hit Kyte so hard that the hulking man dropped to the ice in a thud. It would become the number-one hockey knockout of all time, according to *Bleacher Report,* because it appeared that Kocur hit Kyte so hard he knocked the life right out of his body: as he fell to the ice, Kyte looked like a corpse falling into a coffin. Kyte lay prone on the ice, and then a spirit seemed to move over his limp body. His hands slowly moved, as if guided by a supernatural spirit, to his helmetless head, where his fingers began to explore his skull and hair, trying to see if, in fact, the man who owned the fingers was still alive.

Then there was the time that Kocur hit Donald Brashear so hard that the victim's pain lasted for days after the fight, the force of the right hand sending throbbing waves of misery through Brashear's skull.

"Kocur was hitting me in the helmet like a power hammer, and in the end the helmet split!" Brashear says. During that fight, as the two men squared off, Brashear had circled Kocur with his fists spastically shaking up and down in anticipation. Kocur just skated as calm as a gunslinger at high noon, his right fist cocked on his hip, and stared coldly ahead, waiting. Once engaged, Brashear immediately tied up Kocur's right hand, and they got into a tangle of jerseys and pads. But then Kocur pulled the trigger, and boom—he landed a punch that hit Brashear so hard it cracked his helmet.

"I remember the next day I had a terrible pain; my gums on the left side of my head were hurting even though he was hitting me on the right side of my face," Brashear says. "I couldn't chew anything. I wondered what it would be if I didn't have a helmet. Too scary."

Kocur was drafted by the Red Wings in the fifth round in 1983 after he spent his youth career scoring goals and knocking guys out cold. Once he got called up to Detroit, he spent his formative years brawling through the NHL with his Bruise-Brother teammate Bob Probert, and they would become one of the most feared duos in league history.

"Back in the day in Detroit, when tough guys were coming into Detroit, they had a choice," Draper says. "Fight Probert and have him embarrass you for two minutes, or fight Kocur and he could knock you out with one punch. Pick your poison."

Probert had developed a reputation as the toughest man in hockey. He was incredibly strong and had a serious mean streak on the ice that burned through his veins like a flame swallowing a wick. He had the endurance to last through any fight and would just string fighters along in a marathon of clutching and grabbing and punching; he reached his most savage state late in brawls when his opponent was exhausted. His fights were basically long, drawn-out, jersey-tearing street fights. That was actually one of his strategies: Probert would disrobe as quickly as possible. His jersey sleeve would get loose, and he'd slip his arm out so he could swing more freely (the normal tie-down on his jersey back seemed to be an after-thought). When Probert got his arm free you had to look the hell out, because off came the elbow pad, the shoulder pads, the helmet, the whole jersey itself, and then he got to jack-hammering with a snarl. His opponents had little ability to defend themselves, because there was nothing to hold on to.

While Probert was the marathon man, Kocur was the opposite. He earned the title of hardest puncher in the league, a man who could end a career in seconds, with just one hit.

More important, the pugilistic reputations that Probert and Kocur had earned preceded them wherever they went. Their dual brutality haunted the minds of the opposition as their game versus the Red Wings approached. Every team that faced the Detroit Red Wings during the 1980s had the unen-viable task of having to try to corral both Probert and Kocur, two bulls without a matador. Probert and Kocur roamed free through the league and struck with impunity, rumored to go over opposing lineups to decide which players they would try to intimidate, which players they would try to fight, which rules were fair game to break (such as hitting the goalie), and which players each had a personal grievance against from previous games and encounters. Their verbal threats and violent antics weren't simply for show. They served a purpose: to strike fear into the heart of the opposition. Probert's and Kocur's malice, their scowls, their cold eyes, their threats, their punches to the backs of unexpecting heads would get the skill players twitchy and nervous and always looking over their shoulders instead of focusing on scoring goals. Then when Probert and Kocur beat the tar out of the other team's tough guys, all hope was lost for the night.

Even the toughest and scariest hockey players in the NHL needed to summon an extra shot of courage when dealing with Probert and Kocur. Craig Berube played more than one thousand NHL games in seventeen seasons, racking up over 240 NHL fights and 3,000 penalty minutes (seventh all-time). From a physical standpoint, Berube was one of the most willing combatants the league had ever seen. He was a solid checker and a sound defensive player, and at 6'1" and 215 pounds, he didn't back down from anyone. In fact, on Berube's first shift in his first game in the NHL for the Philadelphia Flyers, he asked Pittsburgh Penguins tough guy Dan Frawley if he wanted to fight.

"In that first game, I had, like, point-fifty-six seconds of total ice time and three fights and about forty-five minutes in penalties," Berube says bluntly.

For much of his career, Berube and his rampaging playing style were like something out of the movie *Slap Shot*. He is part Cree, one of the largest groups of First Nations or Native Americans in North America, and he was known league-wide simply by the nickname "Chief." With numerous teeth knocked out, he looked like a jack-o'-lantern with fangs, and his nose had been broken and set so many times it had a knot on the bridge. When his hockey helmet got ripped off in a fight, it exposed a glorious black mullet that was its own helmet of hair. One time when Berube was in a heated fight with Lindy Ruff, the two referees tried to separate them. Berube got an arm loose and swung at Ruff but instead ended up coldcocking one of the linesmen. With on-ice antics like that, Berube became the stuff of legend. But even he had his limits.

"I got called up from the minors and had to deal with . . . all that," Berube says, chuckling at the absurdity of facing Probert and Kocur as a rookie with the Philadelphia Flyers.

IN HIS FIRST WEEK in the NHL, Berube fought the combo of Probert and Kocur an astonishing four times in two games. In the first game of a home-and-home series in Philadelphia, Berube first fought Probert. He cut Probert over the nose, which was both a good and bad thing. On one hand, everyone noticed that Berube, the young buck, had struck the big bull, and he was called out in an emphatic way. On the other hand, though, you don't beat the bull without the bull becoming enraged.

Berube's first fight with Probert was the typical bout that left the ice surface resembling a yard sale of discarded goods. As the two combatants sat in the penalty box snorting with adrenaline, they watched the other players and referees clean up the refuse.

"Back then there was no glass covering the penalty box door," Berube says. "So Kocur was out there on the ice picking up all of Probert's stuff. He throws the gloves and pads and helmet into the penalty box for Probert. Then Kocur skates right up to me and through the open penalty box says, 'I'm next.' So I had to sit in there for five minutes and think about fighting Kocur after I just fought Probert. And sure enough, I get out of the box and I had to fight Kocur."

The second game was in Detroit a day later.

"Berube fought Probert in Philly and beat him pretty good," says Rick Tocchet, one of Berube's young teammates and a fellow scrapper. "We had the back-to-back. So Berube knew Probert was going to fight him when we got back to Detroit. Berube was my roommate, and he was nervous because he knew he had to go again."

In Detroit, the Flyers were sitting in the locker room preparing for the game when head coach Mike Keenan blew in and informed the team that forward Dave Brown, a veteran heavyweight fighter who could easily handle both Probert and Kocur, wasn't going to play. This left Berube and Tocchet having to deal with the bruising antics of Probert and Kocur.

"I'm sitting there thinking, Are you kidding me? We're coming into Detroit and Brownie's not playing, and I gotta go out there and deal with this?" Berube says.

But Brown knew that the young Berube was up to the task.

"Chief was as tough as anyone that ever played the game," Brown says. "He wasn't afraid of anybody. I think Chief gave Probert as much as he could handle if he didn't beat him."

In Detroit, though, things went from bad to worse when Tocchet got tangled up during the opening minutes of the game.

"Well, on my first shift I got an instigator and fought Rick Zombo and got kicked out," Tocchet says, laughing. "As I'm getting kicked out and leaving the ice, Berube, my own teammate, was yelling at me from the bench, all mad because now he had no help. I didn't mean to get kicked out. I just got kicked out."

Berube sat there stewing on the Flyers' bench in a deep hole of solitary confinement, the only Flyer tough guy ready to take on Probert and Kocur—a lot of meat for one young man to handle. Berube quickly learned that there truly is no hiding in the NHL.

Sure enough, on Berube's first shift it was go time, do or die. Probert deliberately bumped thorny Flyer goalie Ron Hextall to draw Berube out, knowing full well he'd have to engage, because if you allow a team to have a go at your goalie in the first few minutes, well, then it's open season for the rest of the game. Berube instantly grabbed Probert and off they went, swinging and trying to tear each other apart. Berube steered clear of Kocur for the rest of the game because he had had enough. But then he fought Probert again at the end of the game for good measure.

That was life for the famous Bruise Brothers of Probert and Kocur during the 1980s: fight and fight some more, let the bulls run free, and make room for the skilled players on the Detroit team to do their thing without fear of being attacked.

But after several seasons platooning for the Red Wings, Kocur was traded to the New York Rangers, who were desperate for toughness to help protect their deeply talented squad (he won his first Cup with the Rangers in 1994). After amassing more than 2,000 penalty minutes, Kocur eventually retired, largely due to the deterioration of his battered right hand, which had extensive ligament and nerve damage from all the fights. After he retired, he was playing in a beer league when the Detroit Red Wings came calling once again, looking to add toughness to their lineup. He re-signed with the Red Wings and was placed on the Grind Line, where he dug a trench all up and down the right wing next to Draper and Maltby.

On his second tour of duty with the Wings, Kocur didn't fight as much as he had during his earlier years, but it didn't matter. His right fist was still a nuclear device no one wanted to set off. The mere threat of Kocur's right hand coming down was enough to give Draper and Maltby enough leash to misbehave. Because of their motor mouths and hard-nosed, irritating playing style, they drove their opponents into wild fits of retaliation and outright revenge. Draper and Maltby faced an untold number of threats from countless players. From meaningless preseason games to the Stanley Cup Finals, Draper and Maltby never stopped talking, never put away the blowtorch, never laid off the hitting and scrumming, and so everyone they faced—along with the fans—wanted to extinguish both of them at one point or another.

"I talked more than I probably should have," Draper says with a laugh. "But I could talk because of the wingers I had. Having Kocur on our right side led me and Maltby. I played on the edge, and sometimes went over the edge. We did what we wanted to get under the other team's skin. When we were playing the Capitals in the Stanley Cup Finals, Craig Berube threatened to carve our eyes out."

At first, Draper didn't move after that threat, because he was at the face-off circle. Then he slid behind Kocur and told him that he liked his eyes right where they were. Kocur simply skated forward and told the Capitals' tough guy trio of Berube, Chris Simon, and Dale Hunter that nothing was going to happen to Draper and Maltby.

"Berube said, 'It might not be tonight, might not be next season, it could be in a parking lot, or it could be in ten years, but I'll getcha,'" Draper says.

"Ninety-nine percent of the chirps were cursing. There were just a lot of threats," Maltby says with a chuckle. "Berube threatened to carve out our eyes. We didn't think it would happen. But he snapped a little bit, and we just never knew."

Draper and Maltby took to calling Kocur "Papa Bear" because of his burly and paternal presence out on the ice. Anytime there was trouble with his two rambunctious cubs—and they were seemingly always into something—Kocur would ramble in and set everyone straight on what was and what was not going to happen.

"Draper and I stirred things up a lot, and it got on the news and under the opponent's skin," Maltby says. "There were so many times when we were in a skirmish and you'd hear Joe come in and say 'Nothing to see here' or 'What's going on?' It was comical, really."

All joking aside, Kocur helped Draper and Maltby survive. Without Papa Bear patrolling the ice, it was open season on the two mouthy forwards. Kocur was their lifeline and allowed them the freedom to chirp their opponents, to slash at their heels, to stick them in vulnerable areas, and above all, to play the type of game that drove their opponents crazy. They could be as naughty as they wanted to be, because everyone knew that to retaliate was to poke the bear, and no one wanted a piece of Kocur.

"We dreaded when Joe got kicked out too early," Maltby says. "Drapes and I had to look out for each other."

But it wasn't just Draper and Maltby that Kocur protected. It was the entire Detroit team. "My job [was also] to keep the flies off of Stevie," Kocur says, referring to Hall of Fame captain Steve Yzerman.

Most hockey fights occur either as a direct response to a big event, such as a hit or a suspension-worthy cheap shot on a team's skilled player, or as a way to spark a sluggish team. But fights can sometimes start with a smaller infraction, which, if left unattended, can become infected, demoralizing an entire team. If a team lets a violent act go unanswered and unpunished, it can be exposed as having a weak backbone. To be a successful hockey team, to survive bitter divisional rivalries, to make deep runs in the playoffs, a team needs to become a wolf pack, one unit that protects its own, especially the elders and elite scoring forwards.

One day the Red Wings were playing the Phoenix Coyotes, and Kocur and Draper were sitting next to each other on the bench. Draper got a firsthand glimpse into what Joe Kocur really meant to his hockey club, of how he stood guard and fought for his pack, his team.

Rick Tocchet was playing for the Phoenix Coyotes. Tocchet was a renowned tough guy who broke into the NHL with the Flyers as a tough scrapper who could also post up some serious points. Tocchet was no punk, though. He played the game hard and straight up and knew where the line was on acceptable behavior. During the game, Tocchet collided with Detroit captain and superstar Steve Yzerman, and the two veteran players got into a heated tussle. Draper and Kocur saw the whole thing develop from the bench.

"Kocur is sitting on the bench and pops up," Draper says. "He points at Tocchet, and he knows exactly what is going on."

The message was clear: no one touches the Red Wings' superstar and captain without paying for it. Otherwise that little infraction from Tocchet could be followed by a major slash across Yzerman's arm that breaks his hand or wrist, and then he's out for weeks or months.

As Draper and Kocur sat there on the bench waiting for their line to be called, Kocur looked over and came up with a game plan.

"Kocur said to me, 'Gotta do my job. I gotta go after Tocchet. I want you to take a run at him first,'" Draper says.

Draper saw the immediate danger in the plan: he was a helluva lot faster than Kocur, and if he ran Tocchet and ignited a scrum, he would be left having to deal with one of the league's toughest players all by himself. He'd take the chance at getting pummeled just waiting for Papa Pear to come to the rescue.

"I told Kocur that I'm a lot faster than he was and if I hit Tocchet, he better be right behind me," Draper says.

The Grind Line's number was called, and Maltby, Draper, and Kocur climbed over the boards. The game was tied 3–3 in the second period. As the play went on, Draper seized his opportunity and took a huge and reckless run at Tocchet and checked him hard into the side boards. Tocchet took exception to the hit and was now pissed off. So he immediately went after Draper, and they started cross-checking each other.

"All of a sudden, I'm thinking that Kocur should be there any second," Draper says, chuckling.

Sure enough, Kocur flew in and it was go time. Kocur still had his gloves on, though, and pressed them firmly into Tocchet's jersey collar. He didn't jump Tocchet or hit him with a cheap shot that could've seriously injured him. Kocur simply started pushing Tocchet backward. Words were exchanged, and he was getting his point straight out: you messed with Yzerman, and now here is your consequence. Kocur continued to press Tocchet and forced the issue, giving him no alternative other than to fight.

Tocchet was a gamer, a man with one of the highest battle levels in the league. While he was never the most skilled player on the roster, he maximized his talents and was a workaholic in the gym. He was highly competitive and had a giant chip on his shoulder. This led him to play an aggressive style against the league's best players, including Yzerman.

"Anytime I would go up against someone, I tried to go hard against them. I took it as a personal challenge," Tocchet says. "You try to be respectful of the other guy and don't want to be dirty or anything. But I did want the high battle test against anybody."

Tocchet knew the rule: if you're going to have the stones to hit a star player like Steve Yzerman, then you'd better have the stones to be held accountable.

During a game in Toronto when he was with Philadelphia, he went toe-to-toe with Maple Leafs forward Wendel Clark, a bucking bronco of an NHL power forward, in a raucous scrape that erupted out of Clark hitting Flyer defenseman Mark Howe, a highly talented puck-moving defenseman.

"Before I fought Clark, there was a two-year run where he was beating up a lot of people. He was the king of Toronto," Tocchet says. "The good thing about the fight for me was that during that game, he absolutely leveled Mark Howe. So for me it was a spontaneous thing, two guys going at it. Great fight. Both respected each other. It wasn't staged or like I was going into Toronto to prove my manhood versus Clark. It was me stepping in for Howe."

Tocchet knew the rules. Just like Wendel Clark had hit Howe, he hit Yzerman, and now here was Kocur to keep things straight.

The gloves came off in a flash, and Kocur's first two punches were quick and hard, undermining Tocchet's defense. Draper and Maltby stood guard and kept the other Coyote players from getting into the mix. Now everyone was paired up as the man with the steel fist went to work against one of the best scrappers in the modern era.

"Those two fought," Draper says, his words once again wrapped in a bit of awe. "I remember Kocur's throwing the first punch and I was right there, and wow."

One right hand after another glanced off the side of Tocchet's head. Tocchet, a seasoned veteran, was as smart as he was tough; he held Kocur close so as to not let the battering ram gain much steam on its way in. But the blows came down angrier and angrier, one after the next, as if the hands themselves were pissed at not hitting their intended target. Tocchet had his head turned away sharply, down and to the right, as far away as possible from the brunt of Kocur's fist.

Tocchet knew the total destruction that Kocur's right hand could cause; so did everyone else in the league. The stories were not hyperbole, whispers traded in the corner of the locker room. The truth of Joe Kocur was scary, and it was real, and it was on tape. Everyone had seen the highlight of big Jim Kyte falling lifelessly to the ice, and that was just one fight in a long highlight reel.

In January 1985, Kocur was playing for Adirondack in the AHL when he knocked out Jim Playfair from Nova Scotia. The punch was so heavy it looked like Kocur was swinging a giant mallet at a carnival. He hit Playfair so hard he suffered a nasty cut on his right hand from Playfair's teeth. In another game, he hit Mike Eagles so hard in the ear that Eagles dropped to the ice like an anvil in water, and Kocur skated stone-faced and unamused to the penalty box.

Tocchet spun and got low and shoved Kocur into the boards. Tocchet was holding down Kocur's right jersey sleeve. This gave him an opening, and into it he threw a solid left. However, Kocur turned away from it, and when Tocchet let go of Kocur's right sleeve to throw his left he was himself exposed, and now it was judgment time. Kocur threw a punch so powerful it made Tocchet stumble. Then Kocur hit him on the side of the head and shoulder, the sheer force knocking him down. The message was sent, an order of protection from the court of hockey law.

In the end, a lifetime of fights left Joe Kocur's right fist damaged beyond full repair. Tendons were damaged; a staph infection nearly caused amputation. His right hand would sink into a bottomless bucket of ice during and after games in order to heal. Kocur underwent numerous surgeries to relieve the pain and the damage, but the scar tissue just piled up until his right fist was a hardened monument to power and sacrifice.

Kirk Maltby

"I actually enjoyed getting hit," Kirk Maltby says unabashedly.

It is a strange thing to hear a professional hockey player say those words out loud. But Kirk Maltby was no normal hockey player. Yes, he was an integral part of four Stanley Cup–winning teams and one of the most beloved players in Detroit history. He was also one of the greatest pests in hockey history, so loathed by the opposition that entire cities hated him. For many fans, particularly those in Colorado, his last name was a slur, one that congealed in their mouths, and they spit it out with venomous rage.

"Most of the league hated him," jokes Draper. "Sometimes we hated him in practice. That's how effective he was."

Maltby was hated because his game was annoying at such a fundamental level. When he went in to check an opponent, he never let up; he finished all of his checks, tearing his opponent down to the studs, and was happy to do it. Maltby would climb over the boards, skate as fast as he could, and launch himself into your favorite player. Sometimes it would be a massive, lights-out, open-ice collision. Other times it would just be a rubout along the boards as he smeared the player into the Plexiglas. But every time he was on the ice, he was always running the players you passionately rooted for; after a while, a whistle would blow and there would be a stoppage of play. A scrum would break out, and Maltby would poke at your favorite player with his stick or maybe put his glove in his face and wash it down. Draper would clear the crease with a napalm bomb of obscenities, and Maltby would continue yapping as well. They would light a bonfire of hate right there in the goal crease or corner or face-off circle after each whistle. Maltby would fight, or perhaps Joe Kocur would come in to fight for him, which only made you angrier.

Unless, of course, you were a Detroit fan. In that case, you loved him beyond measure.

"I always enjoyed the physical aspect of the game," Maltby says. "The chirping part was just our personalities, and we knew that it got under their skins. After a playoff series, five or six games and you're constantly finishing checks on players and chirping and giving them a shot in the back of the leg—whatever it may be—it gets to them."

Maltby's job was to stir his opponent into fits, and it wasn't about one individual. The Grind Line went after the whole team, and especially loved going after defensemen.

"We made a point of finishing our checks on the defense and made their game as hard as possible," Maltby says. "Especially at the tail end of a season, if it was going to be a team that we'd play in the first round or second round of the playoffs, we let them know what they were going to get."

What the Grind Line had to give their opponent is what military historians call total war, an all-out guerrilla campaign of physical and mental and spiritual warfare. Nothing was to be left standing when they were done. They burned it all down like Sherman marching to the sea.

They were willing to sacrifice everything they had to win. Consider the time Maltby single-handedly took on the Death Star of slap shots.

When asked if he can recall a time when a teammate sacrificed his body for the good of the team, Kris Draper replies without hesitation. "The time that Maltby stood there and blocked Al MacInnis's slap shot stands out."

The Red Wings were playing St. Louis, and the Blues were on a power play. Maltby was covering the point, where Al MacInnis, a player known throughout the league for wielding the hardest slap shot, which routinely exceeded 100 mph and broke equipment, bones, and the will of penalty killers, was positioned.

When there is a traditional power play, one team has a man advantage and the defending team deploys a penalty-killing unit to stave off the offensive attempts. While the power-play unit features five offensively skilled players, the penalty-kill unit is typically composed of two defensemen, who are positioned near the goal, and two forwards at the top of the offensive zone, up by the blue line. While the defensemen are responsible for clearing the goal crease and controlling traffic near the net, the penalty-killing forwards are responsible for closing down shooting and passing lanes. As a result, they stand directly in the line of fire of the league's best shooters, and it is one of the most dangerous jobs in all of hockey. Penalty-killing forwards like Maltby must willingly hurl themselves in front of slap shots in an attempt to keep the puck from reaching the net. And all the pads in the world can't save them, because the puck always hurts.

"MacInnis's first shot broke Maltby's stick," Draper says. "But then the puck went back to MacInnis and he shot again. That next slap shot hit Maltby in the skate!"

When a player attempts to block a shot, it's best to get his pads squared up and all in line, because this offers the greatest surface area of protection. One of the most vulnerable places to take a slap shot, though, is in the skates. The thick leather of the skate boot may feel sturdy, but in reality boots offer minimal protection against a slap shot. Players often break ankles, toes, or feet. Maltby knew all of this, of course, and still stared down MacInnis's blast. The vulcanized rubber traveling over 100 mph hit his foot dead-on and instantly hobbled him. But hockey games don't stop just because a player may have broken a foot. The Blues' power play cycled on.

The puck swung around the offensive zone, and Maltby, undeterred by the two previous cannon shots, prepared for more. Without a stick and with his foot badly injured, possibly broken, he continued to relentlessly push off on his one good leg and pursue the puck up near the point. The puck came back around to his area, and Maltby remarkably flung himself in front of another shot. He blocked the next slap shot with his hand. By the end of the power play, Maltby had blocked three shots with his body and was seen limping to the bench, visibly battered but lifted emotionally by the chanting Detroit crowd.

"I had to put ice bags on my ankles on the bench after that," Maltby says, shrugging it off. "It is never fun blocking shots. It's part of the job."

In another game, MacInnis was teeing off another slap shot when Maltby once again got to work and stepped directly into harm's way.

"He shattered the toe cap on my skate," Maltby says. "I thought he broke my entire foot and all my toes. When I got to the dressing room to change my skate, three of my toes were instantly black-and-blue. I don't know how he didn't break them."

Maltby was X-rayed, and when the films came back negative, the Detroit equipment men put a replacement skate on his foot and he went back out there.

But life on the Red Wings during those dominant years in the 1990s and early 2000s was like that. The Red Wing players were all in, no matter their status or career stats or role.

"In the '98 playoffs, my teammate Brent Gilchrist was getting shot up in the groin and stomach area," Maltby says. "It was for his groin and sports hernia. It was a disaster in his abdomen."

The Red Wings were on the road in the old Dallas arena, playing the Stars. Gilchrist would leave the dressing room and go out into another room with the doctors to receive his shots.

"He was biting down on stuff, and we could hear him wincing and moaning out in the hallway," Maltby says. "Gilchrist was getting it every . . . single . . . game. He couldn't play in the finals because it was just too much. We were so happy to win the Cup for a guy like him."

Sometimes doing everything for the team crossed the line of player etiquette and entered barbarism. This happened in the rivalry between the Colorado Avalanche and the Red Wings, one full of political chess moves, verbal sparring in the newspapers, cheap shots, and the acquisition of players for muscle or for stick work. The entire war was ignited by the Lemieux hit on Draper; the ensuing violence lasted several years and yielded some horrific bloodshed.

In 1997, things took a turn toward the medieval during a fight between Colorado's René Corbet and Detroit's Brendan Shanahan. It was during the Western Conference Finals; the Red Wings were up two games to one in the series and were leading 6–0 in the third period of Game 4. The Red Wings' Martin Lapointe hit Eric Lacroix with a hip check near his knees, and a massive scrum broke out. Shanahan fought Corbet and worked him over with a serious of heavy rights, eventually throwing him to the ice. As the players paired up and stood around, Shanahan lay on top of Corbet. Then Corbet's legs started twitching and he began flailing about on the ice. Soon there was blood all over the place.

"Corbet had a cut in his cheek and it was stitched up," Maltby says. "They got into a fight. Shannie [Shanahan] told us afterwards that he grabbed it and ripped it open."

Tearing open another man's stitches may be over the line (I guess it depends on whether you live in Colorado or Michigan), but physical, gutsy hockey has always been in Maltby's wheelhouse. Long before he ever made it to the NHL, toughness was ingrained in him.

"My parents were a huge part [of learning to play in pain]," Maltby says. "They set in me the hard work. They didn't miss a day of work even when they were sick. They had to be on their deathbed before they'd miss work. I remember one time my mom was sick and I needed something for hockey. She was sick, and Dad was at work, and she still took me. She had to pull over because she wasn't feeling good. When you grow up with things like that, it gets instilled in you."

Maltby was around sacrifice all the time at home and at the rink. He remembers his dad hitting his thumb with a hammer and then duct-taping the wound closed and carrying on. At the rink it was no different. Physicality was a natural part of hockey to him. As he grew up, the injuries, the bumps, the bruises, grew with him, too. When he was a young player he was whacked, punched, hit into the boards, and, yes, hit in the foot with flying pucks. Kirk Maltby simply grew accustomed to it all from an early age.

"It all hurts the same at any age and any level," Maltby says.

When pressed about any particular injuries that stand out, Maltby gives a good-natured shrug. He doesn't want to draw too much attention to what he considers to be minor injuries, especially given players like Gilchrist, who was biting down and receiving shots just to play, and Draper, whose crushed face he saw up close. But after a thousand games in the NHL, Maltby knows what real pain looks and feels like.

He says, almost as an afterthought, "At the end of my career, my shoulder was so busted I could not raise my arm to get my jersey on. Oh, I once got hit so hard in the head my visor broke in half and the bone in my nose stuck out."

Maltby doesn't elaborate any further because he feels there is no need. For the members of the Grind Line, bones puncturing skin was all just a part of their job, of playing the game, of killing all those penalties, of laying down their bodies for the good of the team. As humble as Maltby may be, no one can dispute the fact that one of the shining moments in his career, and ultimately in the history of the Grind Line, was when he willingly and repeatedly stepped in front of MacInnis's slap shot, a cannon that scattered lesser men like dandelion seeds in the wind. But not him. He laid it all down.

"At the young level, I never shied away from it. I didn't want to get my head taken off. But hitting got me involved, got me going, got the adrenaline going," Maltby says. He pauses and then adds without any second thought, "I actually enjoyed getting hit."

Darren McCarty

In the 1996–97 NHL season, the road to the Stanley Cup went through Denver, Colorado. The Avalanche, the defending champions and looking to repeat, were a star-studded squad with an elite goaltender, Patrick Roy; world-class forwards Joe Sakic and Peter Forsberg; stout defenseman Adam Foote; and belt sander extraordinaire Shjon Podein. There were no real chinks in their armor. The Red Wings knew it, too. During that season Detroit was a desperate animal, hungry and cornered. The Red Wings simply could not beat Colorado. The champion Avalanche were still clearly the better team: so far in the 1996–97 regular season they had beaten Detroit all three times they faced them (a 4–1 decision in November, 4–3 in December, and 4–2 in March).

Hockey games, especially playoff games, are all about momentum: when to push it, when to hold on to it, and when to steal some back. Detroit was making no progress against Colorado and in fact was losing ground on their nemesis. If they were unable to beat Colorado in the regular season, they knew that the Avalanche would, more than likely, drive right over them in the playoffs once again.

Then came March 26, 1997, now known as "Bloody Wednesday" in the historic rivalry between the Colorado Avalanche and Detroit Red Wings. It was more than just a vicious retaliation against a bitter rival, though. It was the day that the Grind Line, and specifically Darren McCarty, dug in and said enough of all that. It was a call to arms for the Detroit players to finally avenge Kris Draper's pain; it was a rallying point to say we haven't beaten this team yet, we're tired of losing, we're tired of getting pushed around, and we're going to make a stand.

While the melee on Blood Wednesday appeared to flare up in an instant, the game moving from a few heated scrapes in the opening minutes to an all-out bar fight by the middle of the first period, the war between the two teams actually had been brewing for years.

In the 1994–95 season, the Red Wings were humbled in the Stanley Cup Finals by New Jersey, swept away by the Devils' workmanlike performance, partly at the hands of the Crash Line, and partly because of the Devils' Claude Lemieux and his playoff acumen. Lemieux, the Devils' malcontent at the time, would lead the playoffs that year in goals and would win the Conn Smythe Award for playoff MVP. Things didn't fare any better in the 1995–96 season when the Red Wings met Claude Lemieux once again in the playoffs. This time Lemieux was playing for the Colorado Avalanche and pancaked Kris Draper's face into the side boards, a hit that injured a crucial player and crushed Detroit's team spirit. After that hit, the Red

Wings would fold in six games to the Avalanche, who would go on to win the 1996 Stanley Cup, led once again by Lemieux.

Things changed in the Red Wings' seventy-third game of the 1996–97 season, on March 26 in Detroit's Joe Louis Arena. The game started off tense, with two fights in the opening minutes. Maltby got into a short fight with René Corbet, his exact double in style and personality on the Avalanche. Then halfway through the period the momentum shifted with the right fist of Darren McCarty.

The melee started when Colorado's Peter Forsberg, a nonfighting but rugged and fearless world-class centerman from Sweden, got tangled up with Detroit's Igor Larionov, a Russian virtuoso who played such a cerebral game with the puck that he was nicknamed "the Professor." As Forsberg and Larionov wrestled along the side boards, all the other players paired up. Rugged Colorado defenseman Adam Foote and a referee got hold of McCarty to try to keep him under control.

Detroit's Brendan Shanahan swooped over and conveniently chopped Foote's arm, which freed McCarty from Foote's clutches. So McCarty homed in on Lemieux.

"I took a direct path toward Lemieux. It was written, and said, that Lemieux never saw me coming. But that's untrue," McCarty says. "I can tell you that I looked him directly in the eyes before I hit him. I wanted him to know my anger. I didn't sucker-punch him, as some have written. I coldcocked him."

McCarty hit Lemieux with a heavy right hand that knocked Lemieux down to the ice. In reality, though, it was more than just a mere punch. For as deplorable as Lemieux's actions occasionally may have been during his career, the man was thick and tough and no paper tiger. He was a stout 6'0" and 215 pounds and could take it just as much as he gave it. But he had no chance of surviving the shot from McCarty, for it was a punch packed with more than just anger; it was a fist filled with vengeance, one that had the weight of his friendship with Draper ingrained in the knuckles, as well as the steel-toed soul of the city of Detroit in its force. Lemieux instantly turtled down on the ice, covering his head with his hands and trying to gather his bearings.

Then all hell broke loose. McCarty hammered Lemieux on the ice and then dragged him to the boards to work him over some more. Lemieux had a previous cut that reopened, and blood smeared across the boards. When Colorado (formerly Montreal) goalie Patrick Roy left his crease to help the defenseless Lemieux, Detroit's Brendan Shanahan cut him off by stepping directly into his path. The hit sent both men flying sideways through the air.

"When Shannie hit Roy, it was like something out of *The Matrix*!" Maltby says.

The game quickly spiraled out of control. Two of the best teams in the league threw everything they had at each other, resulting in ten fights, 144 penalty minutes, and endless stoppages and skirmishes. Obscured by the fury and the bloodlust was the fact that the Red Wings finally beat the Avalanche for the first time all season, a 6–5 overtime win, with the winning goal scored by—you guessed it—Darren McCarty.

"No one knew what was going to begin after the hit on Drapes," Maltby says. "People think we planned it. But there was never a discussion. We thought maybe there'd be a fight. To escalate to the level it did, not only was it a lot of fun to be a part of but it was great for hockey."

"This game wasn't just about me settling up with Lemieux. It was about the Red Wings making the Avalanche understand that we were ready to do whatever it took to run them over en route to a championship," McCarty says. "This was the game when we realized who we were and what we were about. Bloody Wednesday was the event that brought us together as a team. Maybe some look at the game and see mayhem. What I see is the Wings standing up for each other. There is nothing that builds team unity more than fighting shoulder-to-shoulder."

With their hits, scrums, and fights, the Grind Line helped Detroit dig in and stop the losing. After Bloody Wednesday, the Red Wings slowly got their footing. With each game they gained more momentum, and they eventually finished in third place during the regular season, with 94 points. As for Colorado, they continued to roll after Bloody Wednesday and finished in first place in the Western Conference, with a whopping 107 points.

Colorado and Detroit met in the Western Conference Finals and continued their bloodbath, with Game 4 exploding into several massive brawls, one of which included Avs forward René Corbet getting his stitches ripped out, and Colorado head coach Marc Crawford climbing over the divide between the benches and screaming at Detroit coach Scotty Bowman. The Red Wings, galvanized weeks earlier on Bloody Wednesday by McCarty, beat the Avalanche four games to two in the conference finals and made a return appearance in the Stanley Cup Finals.

Because of the throttle-down attitude and play of the Grind Line, Detroit, for the first time in years, carried real momentum and a sense of destiny into the 1997–98 finals. And they would need every ounce of magic and grit and speed that they could gather. The Red Wings played the Philadelphia Flyers, the heaviest team in NHL history, a team that could outmuscle every lineup in the league. The Flyers wielded the Legion of Doom Line, a beefy trio of Eric Lindros, John LeClair, and Mikael Renberg that wreaked havoc on the entire league. But Bowman's faith in the Grind Line was as steadfast as ever. In Game 1 on the road in Philadelphia, Bowman got out his pry bar (Draper), nail gun (Maltby), and hammer (Kocur), and chose to start the Grind Line versus the Legion of Doom Line. The message was loud and clear: Detroit, and the Grind Line, would not back down.

The Flyers were licking their chops at the thought of deep-fried Wings. But the Grind Line stepped right up to the bullies and hit them with their own unique blend of grit, nastiness, knack for scoring, and puck possession skills (over the course of the playoffs the Grind Line contributed 24 points). In the finals, despite being outweighed and outsized, the Grind Line would effectively neuter the Legion of Doom, the highest-scoring line in the league.

The Grind Line scored the first goal of the 1996–97 finals, a shorthanded goal by Maltby, assisted by Draper. Then big bad Joey Kocur got into the scoring mix in Game 1 with a breakaway backhander that went top shelf over Flyer goalie Ron Hextall and showed that he had some sweet sauce in his mitts and not just C4 explosives. The series' backbreaker came in Game 2 when Maltby fired a fifty-foot slap shot for the game winner, assisted by Kocur.

Up three games to zero in the series and back on home ice in Detroit, the Red Wings went out to win it all. In the closing minutes of the first period, Maltby dug the puck out of the side boards and crossed into the slot. He slipped a pass back to Detroit defenseman Nicklas Lidstrom at the point. With Draper and Kocur circling the net, Lidstrom fired in a slap shot for the first goal.

With seven minutes left in the second period in Game 4, McCarty caught the puck at mid-ice, skated through the neutral zone, and found himself one-on-one against Flyers defenseman Janne Niinimaa. McCarty skated straight ahead, almost casually, and as he crossed the offensive blue line he faked to his right on his forehand. But then he cut sharply back across Niinimaa toward his backhand, and soon the Flyer defenseman was crossed up, nothing more than an orange pylon with flailing arms. With the puck now on his backhand, McCarty danced around Niinimaa and came in on Flyer goalie Ron Hextall. In a swift power move, McCarty swept the puck back across the crease to his forehand and left Hextall gasping. Now there was nothing but an empty net, and McCarty tucked the puck in nice and snug, putting the Detroit drought to bed forever. McCarty, a burly, brawling man, spun in celebration, the chains of failure flung off his team.

In a beautiful moment of symmetry, with the Detroit Red Wings up 2–0 in Game 4 and the Detroit crowd rocking with their white pom-poms at the thought of their first Cup in forty-two years, Detroit coach Scotty Bowman made his move to end the drought. Out came Kris Draper, Kirk Maltby, and Joe Kocur.

It was a strategic defensive move. But I also believe that Bowman was honoring the men who were hockey strong in ways that went far beyond the score sheet. These were the men he trusted, the men who had worked so hard in the trenches, fought back from horrendous injuries, jumped in front of cannonballs, heard their names used as slurs in arenas all over the league, and fought endlessly for their teammates, sacrificing their bodies in the process. The Grind Line was at their best when they were acting their worst, when they were pushing and hitting and fighting and agitating, but they also scored huge goals. They won games and playoff series and now had the chance to win it all.

Most of all, they could be trusted to close out games, to be steadfast in their hustle, to keep the throttle down and go all the way until the horn blew. So, in the closing minutes, with the Flyers pressing for goals, the Grind Line, covered in blood for years and now seeking platinum silver, climbed over the boards and got to work.

CHAPTER FOUR
CHRIS NILAN

The group of teenagers who bullied Phoebe Prince in 2009–10 in South Hadley, Massachusetts, drew Chris Nilan out to the fight. Prince, fifteen years old and a native of County Clare in Ireland, had moved to America for a fresh start after suffering from mental health issues on the Emerald Isle and was a freshman at South Hadley High School in the quaint New England hamlet. After her relationship with a popular senior athlete ended, an extensive period of bullying began. Over three months Prince endured a campaign of taunts, texts, and social media. Eventually the bullying became too much to bear, and in January 2010 she hung herself in a stairwell. Her body was sent back to her father in Ireland.

For Chris Nilan, who spent thirteen seasons in the NHL defending his teammates from the bullies of the hockey world, the deaths of Phoebe Prince and countless other kids were too much for him to ignore. After all, he's no patsy, a man waiting for someone else to step in. Chris Nilan does the stepping. He felt that he needed to get in the game and set things straight, just as he had so many times before during his hockey career.

"There were five girls in Massachusetts who bullied Phoebe Prince, and she hung herself," Nilan says bluntly, reached by phone as he boards a Montreal Canadiens alumni bus on his way to play in a charity game. "There was a boy in Ottawa named Jamie Hubley who was a figure skater. It was fucking hockey players who were picking on him, and he committed suicide. I thought I could try to educate and empower and give kids some confidence, and maybe reach some kids."

Nilan was so affected by the Hubley suicide that he got directly involved and participated in an antibullying television advertisement. In the television spot, Nilan sits stoically before a single camera, his soulful Irish eyes staring straight ahead. The fifty-seven-year-old Nilan is still very much a hard man from a hard world, and his rugged and craggy face has the marks to prove it. The TV spot gets to the point quickly.

"I'm Chris Nilan," he says in a serious and deliberate tone straight into the camera. "I'm a former NHL player for the Montreal Canadiens, Boston Bruins, and New York Rangers."

As he speaks about bullying, Nilan wields his words, short and direct, the same way he used to throw his fists on the streets of his Boston youth and on the ice during his professional hockey career.

"The recent tragic death of Jamie Hubley from Ottawa was the result of cruel treatment and constant bullying," Nilan says to the camera. "The next time you or someone else is bullied, please stand up for yourself or for that other person. Bullying is not cool. It is cruel."

At the end of the video, Nilan's eyes remain locked in, never moving off target. He calmly holds up the inside of his left hand, a hand that has been stiffened over the years from arthritis, the end result of a career and life spent punching faces and hockey helmets. But now his battered hand is being raised as a sign of peace, a helping hand extended to try to end the suffering of children everywhere. Inside his open palm, the words "No More Bullies" are poignantly scrawled.

After the Phoebe Prince and Jamie Hubley tragedies, Nilan started a campaign called No More Bullies, run from his website, KnucklesNilan.com. Nilan sells No More Bullies merchandise and donates a portion of the profits to outreach organizations for kids in need. More important, he routinely gives antibullying presentations in schools and community centers all over North America. His speeches are filled with positive messages that empower both children and school staff to help try to eliminate bullying. Several times a month, Nilan stands before a cluster of squirrelly students, microphone in hand, every eye turned toward him, and delivers a fiery and unyielding message about bullies and how they try to force their will and their way on others through intimidation and aggression. His brusque words, delivered in his thick Boston accent, hit just as hard as his right cross used to.

In theory, a former NHL player nicknamed "Knuckles" would not be the ideal candidate to speak to a room full of children about violence both verbal and physical. After all, Nilan was a player renowned for his many acts of on-ice mayhem, a powder keg on skates who amassed over 3,000 penalty minutes and 220 fights in 688 games.

But, in reality, Nilan is the perfect person to speak out on the dangers of bullying.

FOR THIRTEEN SEASONS IN the NHL, his involvement in the fight, his willingness to step in and sacrifice for his teammates, was the single greatest identifiable strain of his hockey strength.

From the minute Nilan entered the NHL, he lived in the lion's den, and every season birthed anew an untold number of lions entering the ring to try to fight, injure, and intimidate his teammates. Despite being only 6'0" and 205 pounds, Nilan never backed down from anyone; he took on all the bullies: the grizzled old lions looking to send a message, as well as the young, rabid ones foaming at the mouth, eager to make a reputation. If you harmed his teammate or stepped out of line, and especially if you bullied them in any way, Nilan was there to step in and protect him. His fights were ugly affairs that featured tight, face-to-chest grappling and the kind of short, savage punches and gouging bloodshed that was typically seen in intimate back-alley scraps and bar fights where the grudges were personal.

Today, Nilan is hammer-handed and bone sore from arthritis, the price of a life spent fighting for those in need. Yet he's still fighting, albeit not in the manner that made him famous and beloved by hockey fans all over the world. When Phoebe Prince committed suicide, it was once again go time, but in a different way.

"You're always going to get some smartass kid who just doesn't give a shit," Nilan says as he settles into his seat on the Montreal Canadiens alumni bus. "It all starts at home. That's part of the problem. Half of these kids who bully other kids learn it from their half-wit parents. The parents don't want to say anything or take responsibility because it's a direct reflection on them. They say that their Johnny is not a bully. Well, guess what: your Johnny *is* a bully, and he's a fucking punk, and you gotta do something about it. That's the truth."

Nilan tells how he ended up in a school near Pittsburgh a few years ago, trying to help a young lesbian girl and her best friend who were being bullied relentlessly. The two girls had reached out to Nilan via the No More Bullies campaign. He went to Seneca Valley High School in a suburb of Pittsburgh to protect them, to pick them up, and to empower them.

"There was this girl in Pittsburgh who came to me," Nilan says, his words pushing forward, driving the message home. "She had a friend that was gay who was being tormented and terrorized because of it. The friend kept all of it just between her and her gay friend. She never talked to her mom and dad about it. She never talked to the principal. She didn't go to anybody. She was just suffering in silence."

Chris Nilan spoke with the girl and her friend, and it changed everything. His words of encouragement and power inspired the friend to come forward and instilled in her the confidence to speak up and say something to help her gay friend.

"My speech was it," Nilan says, without a hint of gloating. "After she talked to me, the two girls went and talked to the principal, and demanded that something be done about it."

But how did Chris Nilan, one of the toughest and, quite frankly, scariest players to ever play in the National Hockey League, after all those fights, end up at this point, helping kids in schools across North America? How can Nilan, a man who beat up so many people for so many years in the rink, genuinely hand out advice on bullying? In many ways, the answer to that is simple and bold, just like the man himself.

Chris Nilan's path to this place of peace, this place of nonviolent resolve, was born out of the hockey strength he nurtured on the hard road he's traveled. It's been a journey that has seen his body torn apart by injuries and addiction and put back together one day at a time. Ironically, Nilan's present life as an antibullying advocate was shaped by his own brutal past, his own personal history of violence and destruction. All of his scars and injuries and memories from his life as an NHL enforcer live inside him, and they have marked his life like the rings of a tree.

DESPITE NILAN'S REPUTATION AS one of the meanest players in the history of the NHL, he was, in fact, never a bully, never used a power imbalance to prey on the weak or fragile. He was the opposite.

"I've always been for the underdog," Nilan says sharply. "I've always stuck up for people."

This was a mantra that Nilan's dad drilled into him from an early age: to stand up for anyone smaller or weaker. Whether it was on the street corner or at school or on the ice, and whether it involved a family member or a friend or a teammate, it wasn't negotiable: when someone was being taken advantage of, he was expected to get involved. It was in the gritty streets of Boston that Nilan's hockey strength was born. In many ways, it was a perfect Irish existence. Nilan has always had one fist ready to fight if needed and to protect those who require protecting, to rise up against the oppressive nature of those in power, and the other hand extended to help the fallen get back up, to lift up those in need. This dichotomy that exists in Nilan, and most certainly in most Irishmen, the one where we find both the fighter and the peacemaker, the sinner and the saint, the poet and the plow, was formed in his surly upbringing in Boston, where loyalty to one's family, to one's neighborhood, and to one's crew was ingrained in him from an early age.

Nilan grew up in Boston's crime-riddled West Roxbury section, an Irish-American enclave that was practically governed by clan rule. He first learned to skate on a frozen puddle in a parking lot and learned to play the game in outdoor ice rinks that sprouted up in neighborhoods all over the city of Boston amid the black-and-gold fever created by rushing defenseman Bobby Orr. His upbringing had all the makings of a Martin Scorsese film: truculent kid, street fights, and a stern dad with a military background (Mr. Nilan was a former Green Beret) who used a hands-on form of discipline with his kids. There is no doubt that growing up in the city of Boston toughened Nilan.

"Just growing up with the kids I did in West Roxbury, I learned not to take shit from anybody," Nilan says proudly. "Someone was always looking to get something over on you."

The streets of Boston were filled with hard men, and some of them were monsters. At times there was no avoiding them. Nilan couldn't even go out on a simple date with a pretty girl without feeling the direct threat of violence.

As a young man he drove over to pick up a woman named Karen Stanley. Stanley's mom, Teresa, was dating James "Whitey" Bulger, a man with a very dangerous reputation.

"Bulger gave me the typical, you know, the way a father would talk to any guy that was taking his daughter out," Nilan told Toucher and Rich on CBS Radio. "He had a gun on his lap. He reached over the table, grabbed the gun, and just talked to me. He wanted to see how I would react. I just answered his questions. What's he going to do? Shoot me before the first date?"

Years later, Nilan would marry Karen Stanley and they would have three children together, and the world would eventually discover that Whitey Bulger was the crime lord of Boston, a cold-blooded Irish mob boss who would eventually become number one on the FBI's Most Wanted List after he escaped prosecution for murder and other crimes and went on the lam for decades.

Nilan grew up in this hard place, in city rinks, in streets full of gangsters and goons, of Southies and Townies and Dorsets, all of them looking to protect their turf. To survive his childhood, Nilan became a hard man, too, but lived by a code to protect those who needed help.

"I was able to stand up for myself and friends," Nilan says flatly.

After playing hockey for four years at Northeastern University, Nilan was selected by the Montreal Canadiens as the 231st pick out of 234 players selected in the 1978 NHL draft. He was shipped to Halifax to play for the Nova Scotia Voyageurs in the American Hockey League, a young American college kid battling the stereotype that college players were wimps and couldn't play the sort of ill-tempered hockey called for in those days. He proved them wrong straightaway. Northeastern had gotten him out of West Roxbury, but the streets of Boston never left his heart. Nilan found his way into hockey fights by never taking any shit from anyone on the ice, just as he wouldn't take any shit on the streets in his own neighborhood.

"In my first game for Montreal's farm club, I played against the Philadelphia Flyers' American Hockey League farm team," Nilan says. "I fought Glen Cochrane, a huge guy at six foot four. Well, I cut him bad. Then all of a sudden everyone in the American Hockey League wanted to fight me, and it took off."

Admittedly, he had to work on his hockey skills to become a full-time professional player. His fighting skills, on the other hand, came quite naturally. After all, he'd been fighting his whole life in Boston.

"He was good at fighting because I think he learned a lot in the streets," says Dave Brown, the legendary Philadelphia Flyers heavyweight and Nilan's frequent combatant in the NHL. "He was a real tough guy, and undersized for the job he did. But he would fight anybody. Nilan knew what his job was, and he did his job every night."

No coach had to ask Chris Nilan to fight. No one had to remind him that his job was to take on the nastiest men in the NHL for his teammates. After growing up in a city carved up by neighborhoods and borders, Nilan's hockey strength was already bursting with a fierce sense of clannish loyalty. Now the next step for Nilan was to protect his NHL teammates, most of whom couldn't fight their way out of a wet bag. During the 1979–80 season in the American Hockey League with Nova Scotia, Nilan played 49 games and recorded a staggering 304 penalty minutes.

The following season, Nilan made the Montreal Canadiens' roster. His NHL career started with a literal bang in the first period in his first game versus the big bad Boston Bruins, the team he grew up watching and idolizing. Along with the Philadelphia Flyers, the Boston Bruins of the 1960s through the early 1980s had a notorious reputation as the biggest bullies in the league. The Bruins would terrorize their opponents into submission.

On one of his first shifts in the NHL, Nilan hit Bruins agitator Brad McCrimmon hard into the side boards to let him know that Montreal would no longer be pushed around. Within seconds, Stan Jonathan, the Bruins' tough guy and resident policeman, was all over him. The gloves came flying off and Jonathan hit Nilan with both hands, tuning him up with rights and then lefts. Nilan got in there and swung wildly, landing a few and taking a few, before they fell to the ice in a heap.

"There is Chris Nilan!" the announcer shouted for the very first time in the NHL, even spelling out the newcomer's name: "N-I-L-A-N, a young man from West Roxbury. Going toe-to-toe."

In the second period, Nilan was taking the face-off draw against renowned Bruins tough guy Terry O'Reilly, nicknamed "Taz" for his Tasmanian Devil–like behavior. O'Reilly tried to intimidate Nilan, and by extension the entire Montreal team, and slashed his stick at Nilan right there at the face-off for everyone to see. But Nilan was no patsy, and he gave it right back. Both players got thrown out of the face-off circle, but instead of complying with the referee's order to move to the wing and take positions on either side of the circle, they simply skated in a parallel line until, finding an open stretch of ice, they dropped the gloves.

"Terry O'Reilly was a tough customer," Nilan says. "In my first game, I hit him with two good rights. He hit me with two lefts, and I couldn't see. He hit me right on the button. Blood coming out of my eye, and I couldn't even see where I was."

After the fight was broken up, blood poured out of Nilan's nose and eyes and blotted his crisp, white Montreal jersey. Montreal's Larry Robinson, sporting an epic Afro, stood amusedly next to Nilan the whole time, chewing gum, mentoring the young scrapper as Nilan talked smack to O'Reilly en route to the penalty box.

The announcer once again made an official announcement for Nilan's arrival into the league: "From West Roxbury, quite a story, he made it here to the Canadiens. Nilan is making a name here. It was no contest [for O'Reilly] after Nilan caught him with the first punch."

It was an ass-kicking clinic by O'Reilly, a complete schooling on how things are done in the NHL, and one that set Nilan straight. After that fight in his first game, Nilan made a private promise to himself that it would never happen again, that he would never again fight that wide open and allow himself to get that beaten. For it wasn't just him losing a physical battle; when a team's resident tough guy gets his ass kicked, the whole team suffers. From that point on Nilan improved his technique so he could more effectively stand up for his teammates. Soon his reputation built as one of the toughest guys in the league pound for pound.

When he crossed paths with O'Reilly again, Nilan was already a markedly better fighter. Nilan set out to exact a small amount of revenge and to inform O'Reilly that his reign of terror was over.

"I'm playing in Boston, and their goalie Pete Peeters stuck his goal stick in between my legs," Nilan recalls. When play was stopped and all the players and referees skated to the opposite end of the rink for the face-off in Montreal's zone, Nilan hung back all alone with Peeters and threatened him. "I told him to not do it again or I was going to take his head off.

"Sure enough, boom, he does it again and gives me the stick," Nilan says. "So I cross-checked him flat to the ice right there in the Boston Garden."

O'Reilly came flying in from the other end of the ice, but Nilan was waiting for him, gloves off, stick on the ice, ready to go. O'Reilly came in hot for the kill, a true NHL lion with a wild and flowing mane of hair and a terrible roar. Nilan greeted him with a single straight, heavy punch. Boom. Down.

"O'Reilly came after me, everyone came after me," Nilan says. "I hit him with a right hand. One punch and he was gone."

O'Reilly fell to his knees, bloodied and woozy. A scrum erupted, and Nilan and the Bruin found themselves dog-piled by the linesmen as the rest of the players squared off. When they got O'Reilly up to his feet, it was his turn to have blood pour out his nose and onto his white home jersey. The booing Boston fans rained beer cups onto the ice as Nilan skated to the penalty box, a hometown kid who had just knocked a beloved Bruin. For Nilan, Boston and the Bruins would always be in his heart, but the Canadiens were now his tribe, and his fists and his allegiance now belonged to them. So he went to war for Montreal, his clannish loyalty as strong as ever.

"I heard later that O'Reilly was fucking pissed off at Peeters!" Nilan says with a laugh. "He told Peter to lay off me after the first period. He said, 'Don't wake him up. Just let him play.'"

Nilan hit O'Reilly so hard that they were both seriously injured. The force of the punch severely damaged Nilan's right hand, and he had a hard time even holding his stick for days afterward.

"Two nights later, though," Nilan says, "I ended up fighting Dave Brown in Philly."

Even when injured, Nilan could survive any fight. He was an exceptional technical fighter who fought with sublime skill and proficiency with both hands.

"I just had to fight smart," Nilan says. "A guy my size had to be able to get in tight on bigger guys. They want to hold you out. So I would get in tight on them and tie them up and fight them the way I wanted to fucking fight them."

His endurance was also one of his greatest assets. He could take a punch about as well as anyone ever did in the NHL, and this allowed him to go deep into a scrap, where he would tire out his bigger opponents. Just as the spirit of the fight waned, Nilan would slip out a devastating short punch from close in that did untold amounts of damage, his opponent's head snapping back in a thunderclap of surprise.

"I just tried to do some things technically to take away the strengths of the bigger guys," Nilan explains. "A guy my size, if you want to fight wide open, that was how you broke your jaw, nose, and something bad was going to happen."

During Nilan's long career playing with the Canadiens, the Bruins, and the Rangers, bad things did happen, both major and minor. One of the worst moments was during Game 6 of the Prince of Wales Conference Finals between the Canadiens and Philadelphia Flyers in 1987, where, as we have seen, a massive bench-clearing brawl was ignited over a stupid prank pulled during warm-ups.

"It was a superstition thing," Nilan declares. "Some of our guys would shoot a puck into the opponents' empty net. The Flyers wanted to stop it. So they all came out. I was in the locker room when it all started. I'm not doing any of that shit. I thought it was juvenile."

But when the entire Flyers team spilled out onto the ice looking to end Montrealer Claude Lemieux's shenanigans and prevent him from putting a puck into their net, Nilan had to get involved. He was, as always, one of the first responders on the ice. At first he paired up with the Flyers' Kjell Samuelsson, a 6'6" defenseman from Sweden who had a giant, slender frame, a long pointy face, and a blond bristle mustache that made him look like the Muppets' Swedish chef. Nilan stared up at Samuelsson and offered some choice words. Then he shoved the tall Swede away from the growing scrum. As the ice filled with players from both teams, Nilan eventually found his way to the Flyers' Brown. Brown had come onto the ice bare-chested and without pads. Nilan and Brown fought a grueling battle, with

Nilan's face buried into Brown's bare chest the entire time. Nilan and Brown were the eye of the storm; as they moved around the rink, the squall swirled all around them.

"It was hard to grab on to him," Nilan says sharply. "He just had suspenders. I did the best I could."

Nilan would spend his whole career in the middle of mayhem. Sometimes the on-ice fights weren't enough, though. He occasionally took things a step further. During one game in Vancouver, he was so incensed after a fight with Curt Fraser of the Canucks that when the two combatants retreated to their respective penalty boxes, they grew even more agitated with each other and kept verbally sparring through the Plexiglas. To defuse the situation the referees tossed both Nilan and Fraser out of the game.

So Nilan and Fraser took their conflict off the ice and found each other in the concourse underneath the stands and fought again right there on the concrete and the rugs while still in their equipment. Finally police were summoned and separated the two men.

You never had to ask Nilan to tussle. He was all in, and because of his staggering number of on-ice battles, his years of brawling, and his unrelenting level of sacrifice, he was a beloved teammate. Through more than thirteen seasons he was willing to do anything for his teammates, and he was the one man you wanted with you in the foxhole.

It's one thing to start and settle your own disputes, because you know what you're getting yourself into. It's entirely different, though, when you repeatedly step in and take the blows and injuries on someone else's behalf. Nilan did his job willingly, but it came with a heavy price, and one that ultimately almost took his life.

DEEP INTO OUR INTERVIEW, I say to Nilan, "I'd like to go through a list of your injuries."

I start at the bottom, with his toes. But after a few seconds, he cuts me off. This is because Nilan's history of playing in pain is so extensive that it would take forever to go through all his injuries. Instead, he just reads them off as if he's dictating from his own autopsy report.

"I've had thirty surgeries," Nilan begins in a clinical tone.

"Legs: I've had eleven surgeries on my right knee, eight scopes and three big ones. One scope on my left knee.

"Stomach: I've had a sports hernia.

"Shoulders: I've had both shoulders done twice. Rotator cuffs on both shoulders twice.

"Elbows: I have chips in them.

"Arms: I broke the ulna bone [the forearm bone that runs from the elbow to the pinkie side of the wrist] twice. I played the rest of the game with it. The first time I broke it I was at the Forum with the Rangers and I hit the goalpost. There was about seven minutes left in the game, and I sat on the bench. I just thought I had hit my funny bone, and then when I started turning green I realized it was broken.

"Hands: I had teeth in my hands. Two surgeries. I had a finger bitten off in a street fight, came halfway off. Actually, two fingers were nearly bitten off. I had an infection.

"Face: My nose is like rubber. Believe me. I've gotten hit plenty of times in the nose.

"Stitches: I've got stitches around my eye area. Say about twenty. Three here, two there. Nothing really bad, though. I did get a puck in the head once, my forehead, from Guy Lafleur. He hit me with a slap shot in practice and I got about twenty-five stitches. But it was a plastic surgeon, and they did a pretty good job."

After he retired, the pain actually grew. The aches in his muscles and joints from all the injuries he had sustained over the years had built up layer by layer. And beneath all that, Nilan had been playing with bone-on-bone contact in his right knee since high school. It was after a shoulder surgery when he was done playing that Nilan first turned to Percocet to ease the pain. The pain medication made him feel all right, made him function and able to get through the day. He wasn't taking the pills to get high. He was taking them to try to be able to live a normal life, to go golfing, to slow the crippling arthritic pain that had started creeping through his body and soaking into his joints.

"I had arthritis issues in my knee, my hand, shoulders, back, ankle, everything," says Nilan. "The Percocet worked for me, and the progression, the disease is such that you've got to take more to get the same effect."

CRASH LINE!

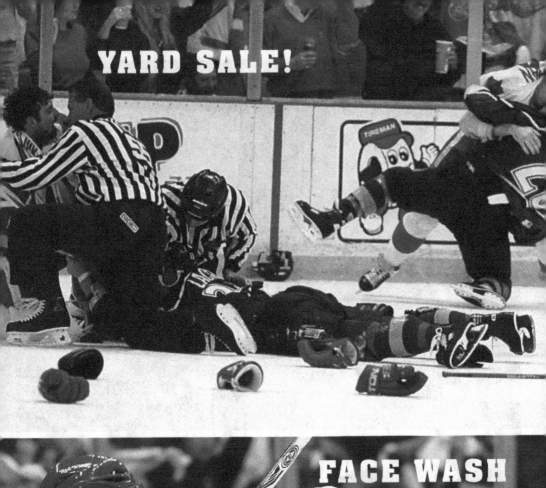

YARD SALE!

FACE WASH

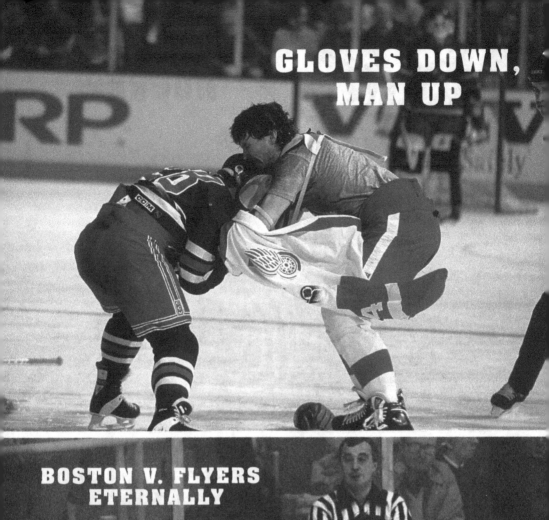

GLOVES DOWN,
MAN UP

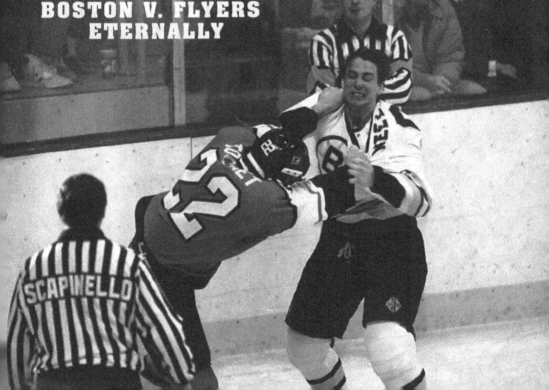

BOSTON V. FLYERS
ETERNALLY

OLD-TIME HOCKEY

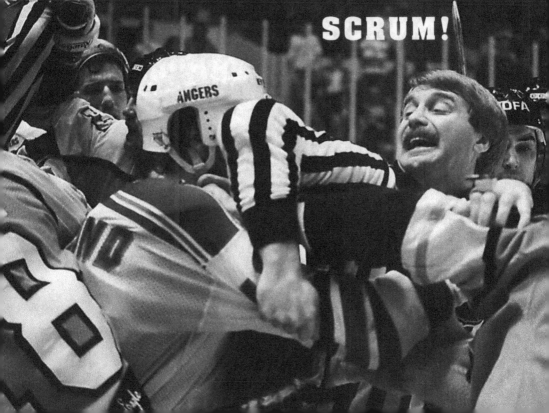

SCRUM!

SMELL
THE
GLOVE!

INTO ENEMY TERRITORY

FINISH YOUR CHECK!

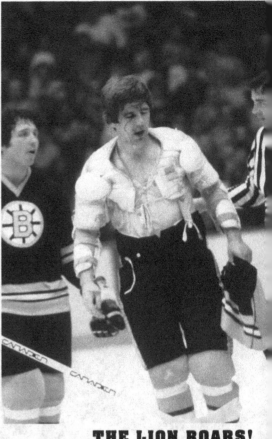

THE LION ROARS!

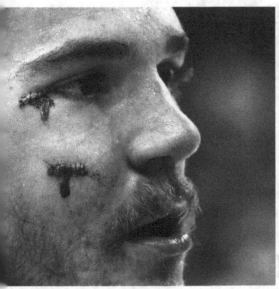

TRADING SCARS FOR STANLEY CUPS

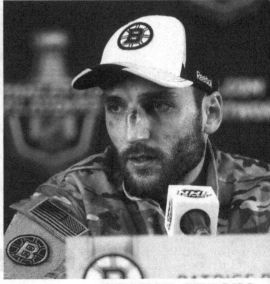

BOSTON STRONG

LEGENDS ON PATROL

Percocet led to Vicodin, and when he couldn't afford that, he turned to the cheapest opiate on the market: heroin. His marriage fell apart, and his relationships with his children and family were sucked into his maelstrom of pain.

"I was just trying to get through the day without hurting another person," Nilan said in the film *The Last Gladiators*, a documentary by Oscar-winning director Alex Gibney about the role of the enforcer in the NHL. It stars Nilan and his fights both on and off the ice.

The blow that put the mighty Chris Nilan down—a man who hardly ever went down—was when he woke up in a hotel bathroom with blood all over his body and a needle stuck in his arm. When he stood up, his legs gave out and he hit his head on the way down.

Soon after, he asked for help and entered rehab. After slipping back into addiction on a few occasions, Nilan is now sober and fights his addiction with meetings and his trademark no-nonsense work ethic and never-stay-down attitude. The physical pain is still there, though; he feels it every day when he wakes up. "I'm stiff in the mornings," Nilan says. "Issues with arthritis in my right knee, hands, and left ankle. But I deal with it. I go to the gym every day. Work out."

His hands took the brunt of his occupation and continue to give him problems. He works out with a trainer now to specifically help strengthen them, which reduces the pain some. His left ankle is not only ravaged with arthritis but once developed a staph infection so severe they almost had to amputate the foot. He had three surgeries on the ankle alone, and that chewed up all the cartilage.

But he no longer numbs himself with narcotics and booze. No matter how many times he's been hit, bitten, or speared, or seen his life dangle at the end of a heroin needle, he's gotten back up and fought his way through.

THE FINAL STAGE IN Nilan's path to peace, the long journey from his history of violence to this place where he has now become an antibullying advocate, was reached when he was finding his sobriety and moved back to Montreal to start a new life. During his playing career he was always involved in altruistic work and spent a lot of time at Montreal Children's Hospital and various charities. Nilan kept hearing in the news about children committing suicide because they were being picked on, and so he harnessed his hockey strength once again to reconfigure his pugnacious playing style into nonviolence advocacy.

In the end, Nilan's reputation as one of the toughest NHL players ever, his Stanley Cup trophy, and his legendary hockey fights and penalty minutes only partially define him. His true legacy is about standing up for others. But Nilan doesn't want any sort of hero talk.

"It's not up to me what I'm remembered for. It's up to whoever," Nilan says. "I just know who I am as a person and what I did as an athlete. I know I could play hockey. I know I could fight. I did my job. I put myself out there for my teammates, and I loved every minute of it."

Chris Nilan has never run from a fight, and he doesn't intend to start now. Whether it's protecting Guy Lafleur on the Montreal Canadiens or a young man like Jamie Hubley in Ottawa, who was tormented for being gay and a figure skater, doesn't matter to him. It's the same fight.

CHAPTER FIVE
DAVID CLARKSON

It's a cold morning, January 1, 2015, and the sun has revealed the wreckage of last night's New Year's Eve festivities on West Seventh Street in downtown St. Paul, Minnesota: Dirty gray snow littered with cigarettes cakes the edges of the city sidewalks, a pedestrian ashtray. The trash cans on the corners have had enough, too; crushed plastic cups spill out of their mouths and lie all around. Cars have been left abandoned and are moored to the curb until their owners return. Last night's revelers are now today's stragglers, and downcast people shuffle clumsily along the sidewalks with their jackets and hats pulled down tight, hooded in what appears to be regret, searching for coffee or a way home or something greasy to eat. The streets themselves are no better. The trucks that rattle down the avenues are driven by the blue-collar folks who are made to work while the greater world takes the day off, and they're pissed about it so they just go right on ahead and crank up the tunes and blow through red lights and say the hell with it.

Then you enter the Xcel Energy Center, home of the Minnesota Wild, and everything changes. On New Year's Day, the inside of the "X" has the sanctity of a church. The stands are completely empty, every row an unclaimed pew, while the massive rows of stadium lights burn with a celestial glow from up high. Underneath the lights a great stillness rolls down deep from the rafters, cascading down . . . down . . . down . . . until it soothingly washes over all the dark-green seats in the lower bowl. At first, the silence is slightly jarring. This arena, voted best NHL rink by *Sports Illustrated* in 2006 with a record 230 straight raucous sellouts, is typically throbbing with eighteen thousand Minnesotans, a fan base that is equally knowledgeable and nervy as they pack the stands to support a team and, more important, a town that is desperate for wins.

On Minnesota Wild game days, the X is your typical modern arena, and it becomes a buzzing cauldron of noise: the shouts of *beer, pretzels, and peaaaaaanuts* pepper the air like buckshot; the metallic wailing of stadium rock peels back the walls and eardrums at nearly every stoppage of play; and overcaffeinated announcers demand the crowd to *GET UP . . . AND . . . MAKE . . . SOME . . . NOISE!*

But not today. Even the famous lighthouse, the shiny tower encased in glass at the top of the arena that blasts a deafening foghorn when the home team scores a goal, stands silent. Right now everything is clean and bright and in its right place. There's not a single nacho tray or soda cup littering the ground. The Zamboni quietly slips off the end of the ice, and the freshly cleaned sheet radiates possibility.

The Toronto Maple Leafs are in town to play the Wild the next day, and Leafs players begin to trickle onto the ice for practice. They won the previous night in Boston, and by beating the Bruins they grabbed a sliver of light in a season that is once again slipping toward the abysmal. Toronto is currently mired in a near-decadelong slump of mediocrity. And this is made all the more painful by the fact that we're talking about the Toronto Maple Leafs here—one of the most storied franchises in all of hockey, a bedrock team in the history of the NHL. This isn't some newborn warm-weather expansion team. No, Toronto fans don't show up to games in shorts. Their fandom is so serious it's ancestral, a provincial allegiance that is the birthright of nearly the entire populace, generations of glory and suffering and rooting for not only the team but the city and a way of life. If you're a Leafs fan, you want the team to win in the same way you wanted to get the girl, a mix of tingling love and sheer desperation and desire and, at times, loathing and hatred.

Due to lukewarm player drafts, the routine parceling out of draft picks, free-agency acquisitions gone awry, and just plain old bad business decisions in the form of bloated contracts, recent years haven't been kind to the Leafs. After a punishing drought of seven years, the Leafs finally made the NHL play-offs in 2013. The city, the province, and all of Leafs Nation once again puffed up their chests and pounded the drums of optimism. Then, in an epic Game 7 in the first round versus the Boston Bruins, the Leafs had a three-goal lead in the third period, and those drums of optimism were pounded like thunder sticks in the hands of John Bonham . . . until . . . until . . . the Bruins, led by their indefatigable alternate captain Patrice Bergeron, scored four consecutive goals and beat the Leafs in overtime. The holy hockey heart of Leafs Nation was once again bereft.

But today they believe. Last night's win in Beantown was a huge one for the struggling team, a positive step forward. Now, in this place, on this clean sheet of glowing ice, fresh off the victory over a loathed rival, anything is possible. It is New Year's Day, after all, a day when people traditionally take a moment to reflect on the past and make resolutions for improvement. This is a day of renewal, and a practice that has been set aside for the stroking of their mojo. The practice moves at such a fast clip and with such precision and positivity that as I sit alone in the vast sea of green seats, I can feel a heavy tide moving out. Even the badly injured Toronto player David Clarkson is seen moving across the ice with ease, laughing it up, hope in his heart that his future will be brighter than his past.

Of all the people who will be in the stadium today and tomorrow, Clarkson is looking for better days ahead now that the calendar has turned. He suffered a grisly facial injury two months ago at the hands of the Buffalo Sabres' Cody McCormick when the two engaged in a spirited preseason fight in October. The right side of his face was clobbered with a punch that left him with two fractures in his cheek and eye socket.

Clarkson knew immediately that he was in trouble when he went to open his mouth and felt liquid flood in. He was seen rubbing his face as he skated toward the penalty box. X-rays in the following days revealed the damage.

Today Clarkson motors around the ice with straight-line speed, hammering shots and zipping passes despite the fact that his face hasn't completely healed. After the high-tempo practice on the first day of the new year, Clarkson stands in the visitors' locker room sweaty and resilient. He sits down at his locker stall and clears out some stuff next to him.

"Take a seat, man," Clarkson offers.

"Really?" I reply in shock. (Note: I've interviewed a lot of hockey players over the years, and Clarkson is the first one to ever offer me a seat.)

"Of course," he replies, his arm extended.

His unpretentious demeanor is no act. Clarkson is a native son of Toronto and was raised in the Mimico neighborhood, where he learned to play hockey in a blue-collar caged-in ice rink simply named the Rink Behind the Beer Store because, well, that's where it was located. He's ruggedly handsome, cut from the hard edges of his working-class upbringing and the manual labor he's endured, and seems like a guy who would be just as comfortable driving a forklift as he is on the forecheck.

More important, he is a third-generation Leafs fan and now plays for his hometown team, wearing the jersey he loved as a child. This is why he continues to battle bravely. Quitting or skipping practice is not an option, because he doesn't want to let down his hockey team, his family, and his town, arguably the holy trinity in most Canadians' lives.

Clarkson slips off his practice jersey, hands it to an equipment man who hovers in the middle of the room, and thanks him. Then he slides off his shoulder pads and hangs them up. A bright green tattoo of a hand grenade is visible on his biceps, and his torso still heaves with adrenaline as the spirited practice works its way out of his system.

"So, how's the face?" I say to begin our interview.

"It's okay," Clarkson answers lightly. "It's the first time for me with an injury like this. I've fought a lot in my career and have never had this happen."

"You continue to play with it, though. Where did you learn to play in pain?" I ask.

"I learned to play in pain growing up," Clarkson says without pause. "I learned it from my family, my dad, and the sport of hockey, and being from Canada."

Clarkson rubs a chapped hand across his scarred chin and wipes a sheet of sweat off his face with a towel. Then he says, "As long as you can play and it's not prohibiting you too much, it's something you want to do. You want to push forward."

Even though he still doesn't have feeling in the cheek area of his face, already nicked with numerous scars, his legs and hands still work so that means he'll play on. He officially received clearance from the Toronto medical staff and team management to continue playing, because they have been able to protect his face with a series of cages and masks. But this medical clearance came with a few restrictions, primarily that he stop fighting for a while. They've advised him that if his face hasn't fully healed and he continues to fight, he runs the severe risk of suffering an injury even worse than before, one that could lead to possible surgeries and rehab and, ultimately, missed games.

"Obviously, I want to play," Clarkson says. "Just getting the feeling back in my face will be something. I have another scan coming up soon. I have to let it sit. The orbital bone is a small bone and takes time to heal. We luckily have really good doctors here, and everything has gone smoothly."

In order to keep playing, for the last two months of 2014 Clarkson tried to adjust to the various face masks and visors that have been attached to his helmet to protect his face. Although the cages and visors allow Clarkson to keep playing with a broken face, they severally limit his vision and, more important, tamp down his naturally pugnacious style, in which fighting and sticking up for his teammates play integral roles.

Now, on the first day of the new year, Clarkson is on the verge of getting all of his facial protection removed, which ultimately means he'll be given full medical clearance soon after to continue fighting if called upon. For most people, a new year represents a fresh start. We look back at the previous year's highs and lows and we make promises to change our ways. But all talk of resolutions and renewal is lost on Clarkson, for he will not shy away from his past, even the very thing that has caused him so much pain. Instead he'll eagerly return to his previous form of fists and scrapes and raising all sorts of hell out there on the ice.

"I'll still play that role," Clarkson says. "Whether it's running around hitting or fighting, I'm going to keep playing the same way. I'm going to finish my checks, and, if need be, stick up for a guy. I'm going to keep doing what got me here."

What got him to the Toronto squad is a playing style filled with aggression and relentless pursuit. At 6'1" and 220 pounds and with an on-ice disposition full of ire (think *Braveheart* on skates), Clarkson plays a game of constant verbal and physical contact. But when there is a cheap shot or other deliberate act of violence against his teammate, or even a small, offhand slight against his goalie's water bottle (more on this later), Clarkson boils over into vengeance and frontier justice. If there is a defining trait in Clarkson's game, it is his unrestrained desire to defend his teammates. On top of all that he possesses a decent scoring touch. He's had a 30-goal year and consistently has scored between 20 and 50 points per season.

Clarkson is going to stick up for his teammates. This is what he's always done, from the Rink Behind the Beer Store with its chain-link "boards" and yellow-painted pipes for goal markers and *Lord of the Flies* rules where he fought off the runts who bullied his little brother and his friends to the gladiator arenas of the Canadian minor leagues, where he racked up hundreds of penalty minutes fighting for his teammates, to the pristine ice of the NHL, where in New Jersey he went through doors and faces to clear space for Zach Parise to his role in 2014–15 riding shotgun for Toronto superstar Phil Kessel.

"My dad always told me to take care of my younger brother, and I did, probably to a fault," Clarkson said in an interview with the *Toronto Star*. "But it's just the way I've always been, whether it's a buddy or brother or teammate. Sometimes it's gotten me into trouble. A lot of times it's helped out."

Recently, Clarkson stepped in to protect a teammate and fought Paul Gaustad of the Nashville Predators despite the fact that he was only a month removed from the incident that smashed the bones in his face; said tiny bones were still very much in the healing process, protected only by the slim guard of a half visor on his helmet.

"It was something where Gaustad hit a guy on our team," Clarkson says with a shrug. He wipes another coating of sweat off his face with a towel. "I ran flying in there and wasn't really thinking about it. When I got into it I was a little protective of my injury. By the end, I got through it, and everything was fine. I wasn't supposed to be fighting. But it happened."

At 6'5" and 230 pounds, Gaustad is a load of a man, bigger and a lot heavier than Clarkson. Plus, Gaustad was all riled up from his fight in the second period against Leafs captain Dion Phaneuf. But Clarkson looked beyond his own regard, his own health, his own face, and engaged Gaustad in a heated, ugly fight that erupted in the goal crease.

In the opening seconds, Gaustad used his size advantage and nearly picked Clarkson up off his skates and smashed him against the glass and end boards. Then Clarkson went on the attack, turning and twisting his way out of the tight spot and punching his way out of his pinned-in position, all the while protecting his right cheek. The fight quickly resembled two male Alaskan bears rearing up, charging each other, and locking up chest to chest in a sweaty, angry hug. Gaustad got a fistful of Clarkson's jersey and smeared it into his face. Major punches were thrown and landed, and Gaustad tried to smash Clarkson back into the end boards. But Clarkson fought him off and punched his way back to level ground. They tied up, and the fight ended. Then Clarkson tore off his own helmet and flung it across the ice, an emphatic sign to his teammates and his opponent that while he was still very much broken he was never going to stop doing what was right.

There's no denying the fact that emotions can get the best of Clarkson and that he can lose it. One example is from 2014, when Clarkson gained infamy for leaving the bench to fight and defend a teammate in trouble. It was during a preseason game versus Buffalo (again!). The Sabres were losing but looking to send a message to the Leafs and other future opponents that they would not go quietly. So they sent out 6'8" forward John Scott, both a likable journeyman and brawling Wookie, to hand-deliver the message via some good old-fashioned goonery. Instead of going after another tough guy, as would be in line with the hockey code of honor, Scott decided to stir the pot to a whole other level and assaulted Phil Kessel, Toronto's star forward. Now, Kessel is a world-class goal scorer, but he's got all the menace of the Pillsbury Doughboy. At the drop of the puck, Scott assaulted Kessel, and Kessel knew he was in serious trouble. So Kessel chopped his stick into Scott's ankle and quickly tried to retreat, but he became ensnared in a briar patch of grabbing hands and arms and jerseys and was instantly in danger.

Clarkson saw the whole incident develop from the bench and decided to respond as he always has. But, as we saw, after the sprawling pregame brawl between the Philadelphia Flyers and the Montreal Canadiens in 1987 that gave the NHL a grotesque black eye in the public relations department— a fight that saw Montreal's Chris Nilan fight a bare-chested Dave Brown—Rule 71 was created to curb the lawlessness of players leaving the bench to fight. In the modern hockey world, leaving the bench is a major no-no and is now viewed as an act of lunacy. But to a player like Clarkson, it's what had to be done. Protecting teammates had always been his top priority.

The fallout from the fight was swift. On one hand, here was Clarkson, a player who had just signed a seven-year, $37.75 million contract to play for his hometown team and was one of the biggest names in that year's free-agency pool. At the time of his signing with Toronto, Clarkson was to be a cornerstone of the Maple Leafs' rebuilding process. But he would now be banned for ten games—and ten games is an eternity in the NHL—which would put Clarkson's development of chemistry with his teammates weeks behind. (The suspension would eventually kill the momentum of his whole first season with Toronto, and this was when criticism of Clarkson began. His lucrative contract in combination with his meager stats, would ultimately lead critics and fans to howl with disappointment. But, note, it's never a player's fault for taking the money. It's a team's fault for paying it.)

But on the other hand, Kessel didn't die. So I guess that's good.

Learning to walk that line of aggression and circumstance is something every NHL tough guy must work at, because toughness and the natural feeling to protect your teammates don't necessarily have an on/off switch. Sure, they must work in a team system and abide by a code. But the rule book can't account for every circumstance, such as when a player like John Scott attacks your franchise player.

W**HEN CLARKSON JUMPED OVER** the boards to fight John Scott, it was clearly a major lack of judgment. No one will argue that fact. But seen through the prism of Clarkson's career, his action comes into a clear focus. In the 2000 Ontario Hockey League draft he was selected by the Belleville Bulls in the eleventh round as the 203rd pick, an afterthought throw of the dart.

He played sparingly, in only twenty-five games. But regardless of his lowly draft status and playing time, he still battled for the Bulls, racking up serious penalty minutes. Then Belleville traded him. For nothing. Yes, that's right: the harsh truth is that when Belleville traded Clarkson, they didn't ask for or receive anything in return. They just let him go. How much would that hurt a kid's pride? He landed in Kitchener, Ontario, and in Pete DeBoer found a coach who believed in him. Soon Clarkson was rejuvenated and went to war again and again for his Kitchener Rangers teammates.

"Peter DeBoer in Kitchener was someone who saw a young kid like me coming in and really made sure I understood what it took to be a pro," Clarkson reflects. "I was very fortunate."

Clarkson worked hard for Kitchener and slowly began laying the foundation his career. He was an aggressive and hard-nosed irritant and shrank from no challenger, doggedly getting up in an opponent's face with fists and gloves and levels of profanity associated with drunken sailors. But when he was NHL draft eligible, Clarkson was passed over by every NHL team in every round. Once again, to know that not a single NHL team wanted him in any round had to hurt beyond measure. But he returned to Kitchener for a third year, a situation that can sometimes be viewed as a failure for a young player, and continued to battle and put his body on the line for the good of the team. He began to smooth out his game, too, dialing down the fighting ever so slightly, beginning to evolve, adding offensive elements to his repertoire. In 51 games in his third OHL season in Kitchener he tallied 33 goals and 21 assists to go along with 145 penalty minutes. But again he was passed over by every NHL team in the draft. The Kitchener coaches had to call in a few favors and landed him tryouts with several NHL teams. After those tryouts, though, none of the teams were willing to sign him.

Nevertheless, the fire in Clarkson's hockey heart refused to die. "It was about me buying in," says Clarkson calmly, his piercing blue eyes staring at the floor as he loosens his skates and then slips them off. "I had the support at home and was surrounded by people that believed in me, believed that I could really do this. Having my family around me when I went through ups and downs meant everything. I also never wanted to give up on my dream of playing in the NHL."

Clarkson eventually signed with the New Jersey Devils and was sent to their AHL farm club in Albany, New York, to play for the Albany River Rats (best name ever) to work on his game and see if he could make it in the world of professional hockey. For all players entering the AHL and the now-defunct International Hockey League, the minor leagues have provided a true test of their hockey strength.

"For me coming out of juniors, the AHL was a jump," Clarkson says. "The number of games we played and how the game was played was different. It was a tough league, and every team had a couple of tough guys, too."

But Clarkson was prepared. He had the rise-and-grind grit of a kid who grew up playing hockey in a cage.

During the 2006–07 AHL season, when he joined the River Rats, they were a losing team. Clarkson got on the bus and went to war in all those arenas in towns like Hartford, Springfield, Hershey, Norfolk, and Portland. He piled up a whopping 233 penalty minutes and 19 fights in only 53 games in his first year in the AHL. That instantly made him one of the greatest Albany enforcers of all time.

"I really wanted to make it to the NHL," Clarkson says quietly. He does not glamorize his hockey fights or any tough-guy image. His role was simply a means to a higher goal: the big time. "That's the way I was going to do it. I was going to go out there and get in guys' faces."

This was how players like David Clarkson and Shjon Podein and Paul Ranheim paid their dues. They got on the bus, bunked in the economy hotels, and went full-tilt physically and mentally every night in the minor leagues. After all, their careers and their dreams were on the line. The scouts from the big clubs were always there, tucked away in the corners of every minor league arena and watching with calculating eyes to see which players had the character, the backbone, and the skill, which ones would fold and which ones would fight through.

Every night was a test for a player. Maybe tonight would be the night the scouts from the big clubs saw something in him that they'd been looking for the whole time. Maybe tonight was the night Ranheim finally bore down, summoned the courage to run the gauntlet through the jousting stick wars in the slot, prove that he was willing to score a greasy goal to win the game. Maybe tonight was the night Podein hustled down the ice, legs churning, giving everything he had, emptying his tank, help kill off a penalty in the last minutes of the game. Maybe tonight was the night Clarkson cracked a defenseman into the boards and then added a couple of assists. Every game was an opportunity to finally make a statement, an irrefutable case that they belonged in the NHL.

Clarkson's travel and game schedule during his rookie year in Albany shows just how daunting the road is for young players out to survive the minor leagues. When Albany went on the road, the team bus traveled through a tangled network of small towns, the strains of endless highways and back roads all tied together like an inseparable knot. It was a long and winding journey. For example, November 2006: 11/3 at Lehigh Valley; 11/4 home versus Providence; 11/9 at Milwaukee; 11/10 at Peoria; 11/11 at Grand Rapids; 11/15 at Binghamton; 11/17 home versus Syracuse; 11/18 home versus Lehigh Valley.

Clarkson doesn't remember one town standing out from another. He can't remember a single hotel he stayed in because they were forgotten the second he checked out. From his seat on the team bus, night bled into day, another round of euchre was played, and sunrise and sunset were indistinguishable out the window.

"I rode the buses in juniors and then in the AHL," Clarkson says. "We were all on there together. We had card games. Guys were sleeping in the aisles. Guys were sleeping between the seats. You just had to keep busy, because those road trips got really long. We'd arrive at the hotel. And a bed was a bed. It didn't matter."

Every player who enters the AHL has a "welcome to the minor leagues" moment, too. Clarkson's didn't come during a game or at a practice or in a fight, though. It came in a hotel.

"We were on the road. I can't even remember where it was. Maybe Syracuse," says Clarkson, laughing. "I'm in my hotel room. It's ten o'clock at night, and someone knocks on my door. There's a pizza delivery guy standing there with ten boxes of pizza. I tell him that I didn't order any pizzas. Pizza delivery guy goes, 'Is your name David Clarkson?' I say, 'Yes, it is.' He goes, 'Is this room 125?' I say, 'Yes, it is.' He goes, 'Well, then these pizzas are for you.' I send the guy away. A minute later, the front desk calls me and informs me I owe the man seventy dollars or they are going to call the team general manager to pay. I really don't want them to do that! So, I have to pay the guy. He brings the pizzas back to my room. I pay him and he leaves. I open up the pizza boxes. All ten pizzas had anchovies."

Veteran pranks on the rookies were just the beginning of Clarkson's education in the minor leagues. On the ice Clarkson was playing and grinding a lot, but he was also enhancing his game, including scoring and learning tricks on the power play.

"In Albany, I was lucky to have a coach like Robbie Ftorek. He taught us how to become better players, how to elevate our game so that we could get to the next level," says Clarkson. "But he had a way of making it fun, and that's what you needed as a player, because the schedule was very tough. You're playing so many games in a week or in a row."

Clarkson looks around the locker room and lets out a small sigh. His time in the minor leagues is still very much a part of him. It doesn't matter that last night he flew into the Twin Cities on a chartered flight and is currently sitting in a polished NHL dressing room and his childhood dream of playing in the NHL has been fully realized. Even though Clarkson will be sleeping tonight in a five-star St. Paul hotel, the one with the top hat–wearing doorman out front, and eating dry-aged, grass-fed New York strip at the world-class steak house around the corner, he knows that one of the main reasons he is sitting there is all those bus rides, all those extra practice sessions honing his snapper from in close, all those lessons learned from Peter DeBoer and Robbie Ftorek and the assembly-line rhythm of the AHL schedule.

"I never thought I'd be where I am today," Clarkson says thoughtfully. "But I worked really, really hard for all of this."

During his second year in the AHL playing in the Devils' minor-league system, this time in Lowell, Massachusetts, he put up 38 points and a bruising 150 penalty minutes. Then it all came together. He was called up to the NHL by Devils general manager Lou Lamoriello in the 2007–08 NHL season. As an undrafted player, he did what he had to do to make it. He survived and hung around and played the only game available to him.

"I was very lucky to have someone like Lou Lamoriello believe in me," says Clarkson.

Clarkson battled his way into the Devils' lineup and never left. In the 2007–08 season, he had 22 points and 183 penalty minutes in 81 games. During the 2011–12 season, the Devils hired Clarkson's old coach Pete DeBoer. Clarkson was wanted by his NHL teammates and was paired with his old coach, and that was all that mattered. He had a breakout year, with 30 goals and 46 points and 138 penalty minutes. Clarkson repaid his teammates' trust by doing everything he could to protect them. After producing solid numbers with the New Jersey Devils, Clarkson became a modern-day power forward, an explosive mix of goals and growl, and signed the multimillion-dollar free-agent deal with his hometown team in Toronto. But all the money in the world wasn't going to unclench his fist.

Clarkson's allegiance to his teammates still knows no boundaries. He's there for his teammates, and he's dug in with his torches lit. This was seen in a Maple Leaf game versus Detroit that was captured on HBO's acclaimed series 24/7. At a stoppage of play, Red Wings forward Todd Bertuzzi shot a puck at Toronto goalie Jonathan Bernier's water bottle, which had fallen to the ice. Clarkson instantly skated over and confronted Bertuzzi about the move.

"Don't fucking hit his bottle," Clarkson said, as a scrum quickly ignited all around him.

"Don't worry about the fucking water bottle," replied Bertuzzi over the mass of bodies.

"I am worried about the water bottle," Clarkson snapped. "That's our fucking water bottle. Don't touch it."

Minutes later, Clarkson was still pissed about Bertuzzi crossing the line, and he wouldn't drop the water-bottle infraction.

"It's our fucking water bottle!" Clarkson roared.

Then Bertuzzi smirked and said, "What are you? The bottle police?" Clarkson let it go, and the play went on. For Clarkson, though, all of this policing of infractions both big and small has come with a price. He has broken his fibula and has been cut so many times by sticks and fists and scrums that he has no idea how many stitches he's endured. In a game versus the Carolina Hurricanes, Clarkson grotesquely tore open his elbow and suffered a major injury to his bursa sac, which acts as a cushion between bone and soft tissue. He received eighteen stitches between periods. As doctors cleaned the wound, blood squirted everywhere, but Clarkson just lay there on his side in his pads, chewing on his mouth guard. When the doctors were done, they sealed the fresh wound in a massive plastic bandage. Clarkson got up and said simply, "I'm playing."

Clarkson returned to that game, of course, and drove into the dirty area of the ice and screened the goalie for a goal. Clarkson battled on for seven more games with the busted bursa sac, but because of his unrelentingly rough play, the injury kept tearing open and had problems draining. Eventually, he had to sit out three games.

"I think in all sports players play through pain and adversity," he says, brushing off any notion of bravado. "It's something that has always happened in hockey. You deal with issues on the ice. Something's sore, but you know it's the best for the team if you can play."

He looks around the Maple Leafs locker room and waves a hand toward his teammates, who are sitting in their locker stalls taking off their pads.

"You see guys on this team have a bad injury or bad stitches and they're back out there the next shift or the end of the period," he says.

"What made me always want to play through things was the players I watched when I was young," Clarkson says. "Players like Dougie Gilmour, Gary Roberts, Wendel Clark, and Darcy Tucker. I saw those guys get hit and get stitches, and they returned to play. They'd be back two minutes later. You watch that as a kid, and it's something that continues in this sport. The main reason we do it is not that we think we're on top of the world. We want to win and be a part of something."

The following night, the Wild and the Leafs square off, and Clarkson is once again in the thick of the action, a part of something. He is a member of both the Toronto team and the Maple Leaf tribe that raised him. The Xcel Energy Center is rocking as usual. The metallic arena rock pounds, and a scoreboard ringing the arena flashes like a relentless digital panic attack. The game is tight, as to be expected, for both teams are still trying to climb out of an early season hole. Leafs forward James van Riemsdyk takes a slap shot square to the face, his bulbous nose turned into a faucet of blood. One can only imagine the pain. But, as Clarkson would have predicted, his teammate is back on the bench minutes later.

Then in the third period, Marco Scandella, a young defenseman for the Wild, goes in for a low hit on Phil Kessell, the sort of hit that isn't blatantly dirty but is certainly uncool. Within seconds, Clarkson flies right into Scandella's space, all fists and fury and fire and smoke, always ready to stick up for a teammate.

There he is, on the second day of the new year, with the two breaks and two fractures in his face still healing, at the intersection of his past and his future. Clarkson has still not been medically cleared to fight, but his gloves are twitching, ready to fly off.

There he is, the son of Toronto, the player no one wanted, the one traded away for nothing, the one who worked tirelessly to turn himself into an NHL player under the bright lights, a long way from the Rink Behind the Beer Store.

Clarkson looks right at Scandella and asks him a simple question: "You wanna go?"

CHAPTER SIX
ROB MCCLANAHAN
VERSUS HERB BROOKS

I find my dad, Gary Smith, in the family room sitting in his favorite spot, a La-Z-Boy recliner nicknamed "the Cat Napper." He is an avid indoorsman (it says so on a magnet on the refrigerator, a gift from my mom) and loves to sit here in his chair, commanding the room and the house like Captain Kirk on the bridge of the starship *Enterprise*. Everything he needs is within an authoritative arm's reach: There is a bowl of cheddary snacks in his lap; his beloved *Dan Patrick Show* plays on the wall-mounted TV immediately before him; newspapers and magazines are scattered on the floor; and an arsenal of remotes and one cordless phone are strategically placed on a table near the arm of his chair. He is a man at rest in all his glory.

But look past his current sedentary life at the ring finger on his right hand and you'll see a symbol of the greatest athletic achievement in the last one hundred years, if not ever. It's a gold band with a bulbous top that's studded with diamonds and represents months upon months of sweat and toil exerted by an American hockey team. More important, his ring represents a moment when the hockey-strong ethos was pushed to the outer limits of endurance and sanity.

My dad was the head athletic trainer of the 1980 "Miracle on Ice" United States men's hockey team, whose monumental upset of the mighty Soviet Union at the 1980 Winter Olympics in Lake Placid, New York, was ranked as the greatest sports moment of the twentieth century by *Sports Illustrated*. He was entrenched for the entire year at the end of the bench and inside the locker room, inside the miracle itself, on the road to gold-medal glory right there alongside cantankerous American coach Herb Brooks and the American players. The ring on his right hand was a gift from the U.S. Olympic Committee (only athletes are awarded Olympic medals). I've never seen him take the ring off, largely because its weight goes far beyond any standard measurement. The stories from that year and those miraculous moments are too strong and alive to ever let go.

Today, I've come to my parents' house to hear the hockey stories that are embedded in his famous Olympic ring. The 1980 Olympic hockey miracle is indisputably one of the greatest underdog sports stories of all time. It is a real-life athletic version of David versus Goliath, a group of fresh-faced college kids fighting tremendous odds and staring down the "Red Army," the Soviet Union hockey team considered one of the greatest teams ever assembled. The "Miracle on Ice" also galvanized a nation at the height of the Cold War and helped ignite a passion for American hockey in generations of young players that continues to this day.

I grew up listening to my dad's sports stories, and they became our conduit, the eternal bond of communication between us. The world of sports and the language it creates has always been our native language, a natural dialect that connects us like no other. And today is no different. I take my usual seat at the corner of a small couch to his immediate left. This is the exact spot where I first heard his stories, and the very place where this book originated. That is because it was while sitting here at my dad's side that I first learned what it truly means to be hockey strong.

Since I was a child, my dad has regaled me with hockey stories. These stories were seasoned with just the right amount of foul language, and the dialogue crackled with so much flavor that they are forever lodged deep in my memory. There were tales of the hockey fights and bench-clearing donnybrooks; of players getting hit so hard they swallowed their own tongues; of folk heroes disguised as hockey players with names like Snuggerud and Chorske and Pavelich and Homer and Brauts; and, of course, stories about all the injured players who gutted it out despite broken bones and even worse, all for the good of the team. More than anything, though, in his stories and anecdotes my dad passed down to me the ancient thread of playing in pain that extends from hockey's humble beginnings to the modern day. From father to son, the hockey-strong ethos was fortified and made into a living thing.

My dad has made a career out of tending to this strength, this unwavering mental and physical stamina that hockey players possess. He has spent a lifetime witnessing world-class hockey at every stage of his career, a period that includes two NCAA ice hockey championships with the Herb Brooks–led University of Minnesota Golden Gophers men's hockey teams in the 1970s, as the head trainer for the Philadelphia Flyers and for the Minnesota Moose of the IHL in the late 1990s, and most recently as the head trainer for high school powerhouse Eden Prairie in suburban Minnesota, an elite hockey program that has produced numerous state titles, several collegiate stars, and a few NHL players in the 2000s. He has spent his time putting hockey players back together so that they can continue playing, because that's what hockey players do.

Today my dad is also going to try to put one more hockey player, albeit a terrible one, back together. I have a severe case of plantar fasciitis, so my left foot is currently in a cumbersome hard plastic walking boot, and my dad wants to give me some much-needed treatment. He's ordered me to stop all activities such as jogging and soccer. But he has cleared me to continue playing hockey because of the supportive structure that my hockey skate provides.

"How we doing?" my dad says as I settle into the couch. He leans forward a few degrees in his recliner. He looks at my walking boot and asks, "How's the blown tire?"

"It's been better."

"For athletes, plantar fasciitis is known as the career killer. Good thing you're not an athlete," my dad quips.

He clicks in the leg rest of his recliner and sits upright. Then he gets up, strolls over, and unstraps my walking boot.

With a raised eyebrow he says, "My son, the beer league all-star."

I reach down and pull out my digital recorder. I'm mainly here for the hockey stories, the ones that have bonded us together for so many years. He knows it, too, because he grunts out a small smile. Despite the fact that he's technically working on his day off, he loves this. He loves that even though I'm forty-three years old and he's seventy-three and nearing retirement, we are still connected, still tethered together by the games we love and the stories they create. I look at his Olympic ring and then turn my eyes up toward him. There is just so much history in his ring, in his workingman's hands, and in his life at the end of the bench.

"Tell me the story about Rob McClanahan, the one when he hurt his leg at the Olympics and Herb Brooks went nuts on him," I say, pressing Record.

With my injured foot in his hand, my dad looks down and says, "That story's a whopper."

"HERB BROOKS HAD FINALLY lost it," my dad begins. "He had finally gone too far."

It was after the first period of the United States men's hockey team's opening game at the 1980 Winter Olympics in Lake Placid, New York, and American coach Herb Brooks verbally accosted forward Rob McClanahan in the locker room with a scathing indictment of McClanahan's toughness. But the tirade had simply gone too far. Brooks's biting words had dug too deep; the American players' emotions exploded like a leaky gas main.

While it was not unusual for Brooks to blow his stack, this specific tirade seemed to cross the line. This was because for an entire year the men on the 1980 U.S. team had given their lives over to Brooks—to representing their country—and had trained exhaustively just to get to the Winter Olympics. The players were handpicked by Brooks, each chosen for specific reasons, and they were some of the most talented amateur hockey players and best-conditioned athletes in the world.

But after six months of preparation, there they were, twenty minutes into their first game in the Olympic tournament, and their coach had lost his mind and unleashed a raw and deeply personal assault on one of the team's best players. In that moment, Brooks nearly undid all the good things they had accomplished over the year.

"Brooks had a plan. He always had a plan," my dad says bluntly, as he wrenches a massager across the bottom of my foot. "Now, remember: Brooks was not only a great coach. He was a psychology major, too."

As head coach of the University of Minnesota Golden Gophers and the U.S. men's team, Brooks was notorious for playing mind games with his players. He had a habit of tinkering with their psyches, constantly poking and prodding them with both pointed and passive comments that were all strategically designed to elicit a response. He employed a never-ending process of addition and subtraction. He would reward a guy with playing time and then take it away without warning. He would pair guys up on lines, and just as things got settled he would scramble them as if they were lottery balls. He would offer up harsh criticism and subtle praise in a single breath.

"He never wanted the players to feel comfortable," my dad continues. "He would motivate them by tearing them down."

All of Brooks's mind games and rigorous cardiovascular conditioning steeled his players both mentally and physically, and his teams achieved tremendous results. He had won three NCAA hockey titles with a lineup made entirely of native Minnesotans and had produced scores of all-Americans and NHL players. Because of this success, his players understood that there was a true method behind his madness.

During his near-totalitarian reign over the U.S. team leading up to the 1980 Winter Olympics, the players were accustomed to the circuit-board tinkering of his mind games. In fact, all the hockey players who had ever played for Brooks had heard him tear into players before. This time, though, was an epic display of wrath, one of the greatest ass-chewings in the history of sports.

McClanahan, one of the best two-way forwards on the American squad, had been injured in the opening minutes of the Sweden game and was eventually sent to the locker room by my dad. McClanahan did not return to the game in the first period after being examined by the American medical staff, and was receiving treatment alone in the locker room.

Brooks, a curt man with as much subtlety as a cinder block, stormed into the locker room with no time for sentiment. The U.S. team had had a lackluster opening period and was down 1–0 after having given up 16 shots to the Swedes. Brooks needed to stir the team awake, and he needed to do it right then and there. My dad had worked with Brooks for years at Minnesota, and the two men had been involved in a similar situation when the Golden Gophers needed a spark in the 1976 Western Collegiate Hockey Association tournament. Brooks's tirade that time included hurling a metal trash can against the locker room wall to charge his players up.

Brooks knew what he had to do, and whether it was right or wrong, he dug right in by questioning McClanahan's toughness, which is a direct shot at any hockey player's character. Brooks knew this, of course, and flayed McClanahan's ego.

"When he came in and challenged me, I was caught completely off guard. Totally off guard," McClanahan says, reached by phone a few days after my dad told me the story in his living room. McClanahan is now fifty-seven and a well-respected and successful financial advisor in the Twin Cities. "He came in and carved me a new one. I was shocked. I'm still shocked today."

AS **MY DAD WORKS** a medieval massager across the arch of my foot, he reminds me that long before there was any gold-medal glory or immortalized Hollywood moment, as in the movie *Miracle*, Rob McClanahan was a solid two-way forward at the University of Minnesota and one of the best all-around players in the country. The St. Paul native had smooth offensive skills but was also a determined and hardworking defensive player. In his three seasons at Minnesota, McClanahan had 108 points in just 121 games and led the team to an NCAA championship in the 1978–79 season.

"He didn't shy away from the physical work and would give a hit or take a hit to make a play," my dad says, his appreciation for McClanahan's game clear. Despite his impressive stats and leadership at Minnesota, however, McClanahan wasn't immune to Brooks's verbal skewers and mind games.

"I remember when I was a freshman and we lost to Lake Superior State," McClanahan says with a laugh. Digging into his memory of his playing days at the University of Minnesota, he can only look back in amazement because of the occasional absurdity of the situation. "For three days straight all we did was Herbies. During that time, my teammate Tommy Vannelli said as we were skating, 'Don't let this bastard beat you.' And he kept repeating it. 'Don't let this bastard beat you.' For three days straight all we did was Herbies."

Herbies are a now-notorious skating drill in which players start on the end goal line and skate to the blue line and back, then to the red line and back, then to the far blue line and back, and then finally to the far goal line and back. The drills are torturous and, of course, nicknamed after their most famous practitioner. But the brutal down-and-backs were only the beginning of Brooks's conditioning. His mental drills were just as exhausting.

"There was always a goal. He always had a way of putting the carrot out there," says Buzz Schneider, a talented and high-scoring forward from Babbitt, Minnesota, who played for Brooks at the University of Minnesota and was a key member of the famous Conehead Line on the 1980 Olympic team. "Herb would always say, 'Yeah, you did that great, but . . . BUT . . .'"

If a Gopher hockey player was rewarded with playing time, he knew it could just as easily be taken away in an instant, and that created a never-ending teeter-totter of emotions. Complacency was Brooks's enemy; he never wanted his players to relax and stay content. He wanted them to always keep working and always strive to get better. He achieved this by alternating his praise and punishment, tearing them down after victories, praising them after defeats, and skating them unmercifully after success. It fostered an atmosphere in which the players gave constant, steady physical effort to survive the turbulent mind games.

"The players never knew where they stood," my dad says. He takes a brief pause from massaging my foot and lets out a small snort of exhaustion. Then he says, "The players were on the edge. They never knew whether they did a good job or they didn't. Win or lose, you couldn't tell."

According to McClanahan, even walking into the locker room for practice was nerve-racking, because Brooks changed the players' lines all the time. The players never knew where they were going to play or if they were going to play at all.

"We'd go to practice, and the jerseys were in different colors for the lines. He'd have different lines and change the lines constantly," McClanahan says. "You never knew where you stood."

DEEP DOWN, BROOKS CARED deeply for his players. He just hardly showed it.

"Brooks was a real smartass," my dad says. "He'd walk by a player and say things like, 'You're playing worse and worse every day, and right now, you're playing so bad it looks like the middle of next week.'" These comments were all by design, though. One of the most critical aspects of Brooks's success was that he was a master motivator. He knew that every player on the roster, no matter where he came from, no matter his background, had his own unique point of motivation buried deep inside. It was Brooks's job to push that button, to get inside the player and motivate him so that he fulfilled his ultimate potential.

"Herbie never did anything without a purpose. Everything had a purpose, and that was the one thing he was a master at," McClanahan says. "In those days, he held all the leverage. And ice time was the leverage. If you wanted to play, you had to suck it up and do whatever it took. Nothing was ever given."

All the players had to abide—or else. Whether you were an all-American scoring machine or a fourth-line tough guy didn't matter to Brooks. He expected every player to come to the rink with a hard hat and a lunch pail regardless of his talent or pedigree. Some players had a hard time with that. The University of Minnesota routinely got the top players in the state every year. Most of these players had been the big men on campus in their respective corners of the state and were used to the privilege of being a star on their little pond, and that meant lots of accolades and ice time. But they learned quickly that Brooks wasn't their friend and there were no more free handouts. He was their coach and teacher, and nothing more.

"There was always a certain wall between the players and Herb," my dad says. "They never came over toward him and he never went over there. Brooks used a few whipping boys to send a message to the team."

As the collegiate seasons progressed, Brooks conducted an ongoing experiment to find out which players were tough enough mentally to withstand his abuse. He was weeding them out, one comment at a time, mentally picking at them to see who would rise and who would fall. And my dad was there the whole time, a crucial set of eyes and ears for Brooks's mad-scientist experiments.

"He had the ability to turn things on and off like no tomorrow," my dad says, still in disbelief at the aura Brooks created in the locker room. "Sometimes after he reamed a guy I would get a nod from Herbie, and I'd know that he wanted me to check on the player. He wanted to know how a player handled it after he yelled at them. . . . I'd check in with the player, see how he was doing, and give Herbie an update."

When Brooks would find those players who were hardy enough to withstand his mind games, he'd use them to send messages to the rest of the team. He'd publicly harangue a specific guy on the bench or in the locker room for not playing hard enough, telling them they need to back-check more or play tougher on the walls. That gave the entire team something to think about.

At the University of Minnesota, McClanahan was an occasional target and was used by Brooks to motivate the other players. Their relationship was prickly long before they ever reached Lake Placid.

"At the U, Brooks's relationship with McClanahan was always on the edge," my dad says. "But after Herb would say things to McClanahan, get on him a little bit, he asked me many times, 'How's Robbie taking it? How's he doing?'"

McClanahan was a player who proved again and again that he could take what Brooks dished out. But there were numerous others who withered under the assault.

"We had a lot of guys at the [university] that couldn't take it," my dad says, his words tinged with sympathy. "There was a really great player named Tony Dorn. He was a big, strong kid from Thief River Falls. But he could never take it from Herbie. Herb finally broke him, and he left. We had a really good goalie named Jeff Tscherne. He was a great guy, but sometimes his play was really up and down. One game he'd play great, and the next he'd be so-so. Tscherne made, like, seventy saves in a '76 playoff game in triple overtime. Then in the 1976 NCAA championship game, we were going out after the first period and Herbie grabs me by the elbow and says, 'Tell Tscherne he's sick'—even though he wasn't sick at all—'and he's coming out of the game.' So I had to grab Tscherne as he was about to go back into the game and tell him that he was sick and coming out of the game. Herbie pulled him out and put in the other goalie, Tom Mohr. That sort of thing could kill some players."

My dad pauses the story to cover my foot in a damp cloth and seal it in a plastic bag. Then he wraps the foot in a heating pad.

"This will give you some damp heat. Like a jungle," he says. "So, where was I?"

"You're at the Olympics. Rob McClanahan gets hurt. Brooks is about to tear McClanahan a new one," I say.

"So, there we are at the Olympics," he begins, waltzing effortlessly right back into the story. "It's the first period in the game against Sweden, and McClanahan got hit dead center in his thigh. I think it was one of McClanahan's first shifts of the Olympics, and he went down instantly. He tried to play through it, but the pain was so intense. I sent him to the locker room to get looked at and get some treatment."

This was a big blow to the American team, because McClanahan was being counted on to play major minutes for the entirety of the Olympics.

"I had a really bad contusion. It was really bad," McClanahan confirms. "I thought I was toast. It was the first shift of the game, and I went to the locker room."

During McClanahan's absence, the United States played uninspired and nervous hockey in their opening period against Sweden; they were nowhere near their potential. They were now on the world stage, and Brooks knew they could play better and expected more. He needed his team to rally, to chase away their nerves, to erase the memory of their last pretournament game, a humiliating 10–3 loss to the Soviets at Madison Square Garden a week before. Most important, the reputation of their country and the American way of life was in the spotlight.

After the first period ended, Brooks stormed into the American locker room. McClanahan lay on a bench in the corner, undressed, his leg wrapped in ice. In an instant, Brooks ripped into him.

"I was standing there thinking that we're finally here at the Olympics and Herbie's lost it," my dad says.

"What did he say?" I ask.

"He called McClanahan the biggest pussy that ever walked the earth! He said McClanahan wasn't tough enough to ever play in the NHL! And all sorts of stuff. Brooks was ripping him a new asshole and was yelling and screaming at McClanahan."

But McClanahan had had enough of Brooks's antics. This was no longer the University of Minnesota, and he was no longer a freshman who had to suck it up. He wasn't going to let the bastard win. McClanahan made a stand, albeit on one leg. He shot off the bench and went right after his coach.

"Robbie had a huge ice bag wrapped around his leg," my dad says. "He jumped up off the bench and stood up to go after Herbie, and the ice bag flew off through the air. They were screaming at each other."

"I had finally had enough," McClanahan says. "I was ready to throw a punch. As I was moving my arm, one of my teammates grabbed my right arm and stopped me." (Imagine, for a moment, if that punch had been thrown, and Herb Brooks, the head coach of our national team, had shown up for the second period at the Olympics with a fresh black eye.)

"I'd seen a lot of Brooks's yelling matches," my dad says. "But this tirade was so much worse because it was at the Olympics. It was our first game!"

The young American team sat there both awestruck and irate at what was unfolding before their eyes. They had trained for almost an entire year for the Olympics. They had been repeatedly skated into the ground by Brooks, had puked right there on the ice, only to rally and skate some more. They had traveled the globe in an endless parade of exhibition games. They had trained exhaustively, learned all of Brooks's elaborate system, and did everything he asked of them. And now here he was, rewarding them by blowing it all up after just one period of hockey.

At his player's counterassault, Brooks simply turned and walked out into the hallway. McClanahan wasn't done, though, and hobbled after Brooks, screaming the entire way. Now they were in the hallway outside the locker room and in front of some of the Swedish hockey players, who looked over in absolute confusion.

"They were in the hall, and the Swedes were sticking their heads out of their locker room and wondering what the hell was going on," my dad says, laughing at the memory. "Herbie turns on McClanahan and goes back at him again. They go at it again, and Brooks continues telling McClanahan that he's not tough enough."

But McClanahan didn't back down. Standing there undressed in the hall, he gave it right back to Brooks.

"I told him that he wasn't going to tell *me* if I could play or not," McClanahan says, his words bursting with conviction even thirty-six years later. "I told him that I'll tell *him* if I could play or not."

Buzz Schneider sat in the American locker room shaken by the whole explosive episode. As much as it hurt to see his teammate get torn apart, he knew something had to be behind it. There always was.

"Everything [Brooks] did had a reason why he was doing it," Schneider says. "He never did things just for the sake of doing it. He always had a goal."

"Brooks was never vicious or anything like that," Schneider says. "But this time it came off real. I thought to myself,

Holy crap. Herbie came in and went right after him. He did it to everybody I know. He could go after people, and he'd go as deep as he had to, as personal as he had to, to get that button inside of you. He hit Rob's button. I think he went past the button."

It took a while for my dad to see what Brooks was doing. But when the smoke had finally cleared, he saw the daylight that Brooks was after.

No one sees things quite the same way a trainer does. Trainers are there at the end of the bench at all the practices and games. They're on the road trips, too, and are embedded in the locker room and the training room, and because of this, they're often the only ones who can truly gauge the mood of a team. As they treat the players for injuries, they not only rehab the wounds but also sense the players' attitude on the current status of the team and their teammates.

"I looked around the room and thought to myself, *That sly old fox,*" my dad confesses.

My dad pauses one more time and takes my heat wrap off. Next, he puts a ball with rubber spikes all over it under my foot and instructs me to roll it back and forth on my arch to stretch out the tendons. Then he pops back into his chair, shovels a fistful of Cheez-Its into his mouth, and continues.

"No one was saying a word. No one knew what to do. There was a little talk when they were in the hallway, like, What the hell is going on?" my dad says. "At first, I stood there and thought, *God, we're at the Olympics and Herbie has lost it. He's lost it.* But then I looked around the room, and you could tell by their expressions that the players were pissed off. The players were upset and mad that Herbie took their buddy down. There were a lot of the players versus Herb at that time, and he used that to motivate them. He always had a reason for why he was doing things. He was always trying to figure out ways to get more out of them. Against Sweden, after he went after McClanahan, they rallied and went out and played better and stayed in the game."

When McClanahan was done fighting with Brooks, he returned to a changed and refocused locker room, one that was now void of nerves and timid players. The entire mood of the team had changed; they had been galvanized in solidarity with their brother in arms. By attacking McClanahan, Brooks attacked all of them. By questioning his toughness, he questioned all of their toughness.

This, of course, was all by design. Brooks deliberately lit a fuse under McClanahan, and a fire quickly spread. They all rallied in McClanahan's defense and were now tied together in hatred for Brooks like never before. Their nervousness about playing in the opening game of the Olympics against an international powerhouse disappeared.

McClanahan put his pads back on and played the rest of the game—and the rest of the Olympics. Even he admits that Brooks was a master strategist.

"He got his players to respond at the highest level and play their best at the most important time," McClanahan says.

* * *

WHEN MCCLANAHAN BRAVELY MADE his stand, the fact that it was on one leg united his team.

"I put my equipment back on, and I was a gimp. But I played," McClanahan says proudly. "He got what he wanted. It's hard to argue with the results." Just two weeks after the tirade, the Americans would discover gold. His hockey strength engaged, McClanahan toughed it out for the rest of the Sweden game on a leg he could barely bend due to a crippling thigh contusion. He occasionally stood between shifts because the leg would seize up when he sat down. In the closing seconds, the U.S. team rallied to tie Sweden, itself an international powerhouse picked to medal. As we now know, the rally didn't stop there.

The American team would go on a historic roll and upset the Soviet Union, the best team in the world and widely regarded as one of the best teams of all time (they had won six of the previous seven gold medals) in what is now known as the "Miracle on Ice."

When the Americans moved into the gold medal game versus Finland, it was, of course, McClanahan who scored the game-winner.

It has been thirty-six years since Brooks viciously went after McClanahan. The fire has been dampened, and the smoke has long been cleared out. But my dad believes that Brooks didn't question McClanahan's toughness and his hockey strength because it was weak, but rather because it was one of the *strongest* on the team.

"Herbie knew McClanahan could take it," my dad says, his words filled with admiration for McClanahan. "In six months, Herbie got to know all the players on the 1980 Olympic team. When challenged, he knew who could take it, who would play better, and who would player harder. He also knew what players would throw in the towel." In hindsight, my dad believes that if it hadn't been McClanahan who got hurt and laid up in the dressing room but rather a different player with a different degree of hockey strength, it's quite possible destiny would have taken a detour, and a national miracle would never have occurred.

"What people don't realize is that a week earlier, Jack O'Callahan hurt his knee in an exhibition game," he points out. "O'Callahan was a great player, a team leader, and a tough player from Charlestown, Massachusetts. But Herbie didn't go after him, didn't question him. At the time, [goalie] Jim Craig was kind of fragile because his mom had just passed away. Herb wouldn't have gone after him, because he could've broken him."

Because of Brooks's constant mental tinkering, he sometimes knew his players even better than they knew themselves.

"Herbie took in the McClanahan situation," my dad says, leaning back in his recliner. "He had a history and a familiarity with McClanahan unlike his relationship with the guys from the East Coast. Herbie knew that Robbie was maybe ready to pull the chute and throw in the towel. And Herbie wouldn't let him do it. He showed McClanahan that he could come back from adversity, and he played through it, and my God, McClanahan scored the goal that won the gold medal."

THE SUNLIGHT OUTSIDE THE family room begins to fade, and the story my dad tells of the time Rob McClanahan went head-to-head with Herb Brooks comes to an end. But the story of the 1980 United States men's hockey team never really ends. It lives on in a generation of American hockey players, in the collective memories of hockey fans the world over, in the mythology of American sports, in motion pictures, and in displays in the Hockey Hall of Fame. On a personal level, the story of "Miracle on Ice" lives on in the ring on my dad's right hand as he passes the anecdotes down from father to son.

My dad is now tired and cashed out. He has a few valuable hours left in his day off, and he wants to use them now to do nothing. So he settles into his chair, done for the day.

I turn off my digital recorder and sit there for a few minutes, wrapped in the warm glow of his story. After all these years, my dad and I are still tethered together by the sports stories we share, by the games we love, and by the thread of the hockey-strong ethos that connects us. He looks over at me while I put my walking boot back on.

"When is your next game?" he asks.

"This Saturday at Arden Park. Eight a.m. Dark versus White. Same as always."

Before he reclines, my dad asks me the one question that's at the very heart of what it means to be hockey strong. It is a question directed at a player's mental and physical stamina. It is a question of how much pain a player can endure. It is a question as old as the game itself. It is a question that does not discriminate, one that was aimed at Rob McClanahan's heart during the 1980 Winter Olympics and has been faced by every player in this book. It is a simple three words that define the sport. And it is a question my dad has spent a career asking.

"Can you play?" my dad asks me.

"I can play," I answer.

"Then you should play," he says.

CHAPTER SEVEN

JACK CARLSON

Turtle Bread and Coffee in South Minneapolis is the sort of quaint little business that could be used for a romantic comedy starring Paul Rudd. Set on a bustling corner in a leafy neighborhood with an artisanal ice cream parlor next door and an indie bike shop with a wily shop dog lazing around out front, it's a setting where an earnest single dad might get another shot at love and fall for a cutesy baker wearing a dusting of flour as she quietly works the hearth in back. With its creaky hardwood floors, buckets filled with fresh baguettes, and air toasted with sugar, it is an idyllic place for conversation, for a connection, for a good solid chat over a cup of coffee.

Into this picturesque setting strides Jack Carlson, a former professional hockey player. But you most likely will not even recognize his name or even know who he is. If you've ever seen the legendary movie *Slap Shot*, though, you know exactly what he did during his career battling through the ranks of professional hockey.

If you look closely, you'll easily recognize Carlson's big-hearted smile, the nose—my God, the nose—and the rest of his rough-hewn face. Your memory will slide into focus, and you'll recognize Carlson's face, and then you'll see two more faces that look exactly like it. That is because besides being a well-known hockey player, Carlson was, along with his brothers Jeff and Steve, the real-life inspiration for the Hanson Brothers, the affable, black-rimmed-glasses-wearing hooligans of *Slap Shot*, widely regarded as one of the best sports films of all time.

Carlson is the man with a true Hollywood story, and he's ready to share it: how the son of a miner from northern Minnesota made it into professional hockey with his two brothers.

Today, Carlson, sixty, is still the hard-charging, good-natured guy he was when he and his brothers ran roughshod over the world of professional hockey. Carlson strides right past the gaggle of older ladies gossiping over their coffee, the hipsters clickety-clacking away on their laptops, and the couple nestled together in the sunny window like a pair of house cats. Carlson doesn't need coffee, though. He doesn't need a spot of tea or a bagel or a muffin. He walks onto this set and he's already plugged in. He doesn't need to go Method on the acting bit and try to inhabit a character's instincts and clothing and dialogue. Carlson doesn't need to get into character or to rehearse his lines. He's the genuine article.

"Todd, I don't need a coffee. I don't need anything," Carlson says, smiling with gusto. "I'm all jacked up."

Carlson's turbo-boosted spirit comes as no surprise. In person, his good nature is bursting with exuberance, and it matches the rambunctious playing style that he wielded for so long during his career. In the world of professional hockey, the Carlson Brothers were solid, hardworking hockey players, and they could play it any way you wanted it. They were skilled and tough, and sometimes sprinkled in a dash of lunacy. If you wanted to fight, sure, they could fight you all game—Jack and Jeff especially would oblige you. At one point, Jack Carlson was one of the best heavyweight fighters in the world of hockey and routinely beat up the toughest players in both the NHL and the WHL. But if you wanted a nice, clean game, why, then, the brothers could do that, too, and would hang some serious points on the scoreboard.

The Carlson Brothers were a package deal. Whenever they were on the same team, all three of them skated on one line. No exceptions. If you wanted one of them, you'd get all three. This was always the case, whether it was on the forecheck or cycling the puck or in a fight on the ice or in the stands (more on that later). The boys stuck together. During their playing days, there was no real way to control the Carlson Brothers for too long, no real way to rein them in. You just kind of let them go and do their thing, and that meant chaos and goals and, on occasion, a little jail time.

Carlson sits down at a table next to a sunny window in a quiet corner of the coffee shop. He's smiling and demonstrative. His massive hands, with fingers as thick as C batteries, fly through the air, and when he sets a hand back down on the table it hits like a dumbbell. Every time. A hearty, rolling laugh, the sort you'd expect to hear from a gentle giant in a children's folktale, belts out early and often, and echoes around the room as he begins to tell the story of his hockey strength.

"Why do hockey players play in pain?" I ask Carlson.

He sits up straight, eager to get started. It's not hard to imagine that he's sitting on a team bench, ready to go into an actual game, waiting for the coach to call his number so he can get in there and stir the pot.

"I think it's a passion for the game," he says. "It becomes a thing where you don't want to let your teammates down. Okay, so you got dinged up a little bit. One of the things I've talked about with other teammates is that you never wanted to leave the lineup, because you never knew if you were going to get back in."

As he talks, his momentum picks up, and within seconds Carlson is hustling, huffing up and down that wing, sorting it all out in real time, his thoughts streaming together one into the next until he's coming in hot and at full force, as if he were in on the forecheck and trying to separate his man from the puck.

"Back in my day, the expectations from the general manager and coaches were there. I remember managers coming into the locker room and saying, 'You're playing tonight, aren't you?' Well, they're the GM. What are you going to say? 'No'? 'I have a headache. I'm not feeling well'? 'I went down to pick up a bar of soap and I tweaked my back'?

"The other thing, too, is that athletes in other sports will tell you when they are coming back. Not the trainer. Not the doctor. A baseball player will tweak his back and he'll tell people he should be back in the lineup in three days. Oh, okay. Three days. Really? Three days. It's not the doctor expecting him to be out. They tell you when they're going to be back. In baseball, if you have an injury, you have the right to get back into the lineup when you come back. In hockey, you don't. You might sit. Especially if the guy taking your place is playing really well."

For a player like Carlson, with his particular skill set—which consisted of a healthy mix of vigilantism and goal scoring tinged with the grace of a bazooka—he had to stay in the lineup at all costs despite his injuries, because he knew management could always find someone else crazy enough to willingly fight through the ranks of hockey. He suffered fractured vertebrae, hip injuries, three shoulder surgeries, and three knee surgeries, but tried to play through. Carlson had nose reconstruction, teeth knocked out, and more than two hundred stitches.

In August one year, Carlson broke his jaw and the doctor told him it had to be wired shut for six weeks. The problem was that training camp was in September. So, two and a half weeks later, Carlson went to his family doctor in northern Minnesota to get the wires cut out so he could play at training camp. He'd been losing weight because all he could eat was Dinty Moore stew through a straw, so he was worried he wouldn't be strong enough to survive the demands of his profession. Still, Carlson was hockey strong, so he told the doctor he had to get the wires out, and when the doctor asked him how long they'd been in, he lied. Carlson, naturally scared about losing his job, told the doctor six weeks, even though it had been less than three.

"The doctor says, okay, and then he left the room only to return and say, 'Jack, you've only had the wires in for two weeks!' You get to the big league, right. Then you have to keep in mind, what's the guy up in Manitoba doing this summer? He's going to try and take my job at training camp. So the passion for me was that no one was going to take my job. I'm not going to lose it. I might not play well, but it's not going to be from lack of effort."

Then there was the time Carlson was playing in Philadelphia. He had ditched his trademark black Hanson Brothers glasses and was now wearing contact lenses. He went to sweep the puck away from a guy and got knocked down in the process. When the other player took a stride, his skate came up and the blade hit Carlson right in the face.

"It hit me right in the corner of my left eye," Carlson says. "It tore across my nose and forehead. There was blood all over the place. It was inside my contact lens, so I thought I'd lost my eye. I ended up getting twenty-two stitches from the corner of the eye and across my nose and forehead. But I went back in. You just go back in. You get stitched up. I probably missed a period."

Game after game, he fought for both his teammates and his job. He played an entire season in St. Louis in the NHL with a brace on his left arm because the tendons and ligaments were so stretched out that the arm would dislocate or pop out of the socket even after doing something as easy as reaching for a salt shaker. He played through it, of course, and simply wore a brace all year, in more than 50 games and while racking up close to 100 penalty minutes. At the end of the season, mercifully, he got it fixed.

Everyone can see the black eyes, the scars, and the gaps in their teeth that hockey players sport. Those injuries are the showtime wounds of the hockey world, the marks that come with a spotlight of attention and an aura of bad-boy bravado. But a blown-out arm, especially one used to fight off the goons of the hockey world, is the type of injury no one knows about. A player like Carlson would often have to hide his injuries and then privately battle through in silence, seeking treatment in the quiet corners of the training room. During Carlson's career in the 1970s and '80s, when knuckles really flew in the NHL and WHL and playing in pain was a regular part of the job description and the surest way to keep your job, there were no excuses, no straying from the old-time script. When the game's biggest stars, the truly gifted ones with their names emblazoned on trophies—names like Orr, Hull, Esposito, and Howe—when all of those A-list talents played in pain, the extras like Carlson had to follow suit.

"It was a privilege to play with Gordie," Carlson says reverently. "He was so dedicated. One time we were in the playoffs with Hartford and we're up in Edmonton. We had an optional skate. Gordie comes into the locker room to get ready. It was our eighty-fifth game of the season. He's forty-six years old. His skates aren't in his locker. He goes and tries to find his skates, but they're nowhere to be found. The staff comes down and tells him they don't want him to skate. They want him to rest, to take it easy. He looks at them and says, 'Never take my skates. Never take my skates. Never.' He just wanted to be out there."

Gordie played without a helmet, and he was going down to block shots. He wasn't lifting a leg or getting out of the way, which he had earned the right to do. He was forty-six and one of the greatest players of all time, and he was going down—on the ice—to block a shot.

"I'm sitting there on the bench and thinking, *Well, if a guy like that is doing it, who am I not to do it?*" Carlson says.

THE MORNING SUN IS now in full bloom outside the window. Carlson begins to talk about where it all started.

"I great up in Virginia, Minnesota, up in the Iron Range. I had three brothers and an older sister. Age-wise, Steve was nine, I was ten, Jeff was eleven, my sister was twelve, and my oldest brother was fourteen. We kidded my mom and dad about that one year off. Were they not feeling well that year, or what? *Hahaha-who-ha!*"

Carlson's dad worked in the mines, and his mom worked three jobs. Carlson says his family didn't have a whole lot, and he remembers his dad telling him to grab any broken hockey sticks they found at the local ice rinks in northern Minnesota. His dad would use screws and nails to fix the broken sticks because he couldn't afford to buy his growing brood of players new sticks all the time.

"He had three kids playing hockey," Carlson says, his eyes growing wide as the memories begin to percolate. "I remember that sticks were eight dollars, and my dad didn't have eight dollars for a stick."

What the Carlson Brothers may have lacked in equipment and pedigree they more than made up for in ice time. The longest season in the state of Minnesota is winter. It's even longer in the northern part of the state, where winter comes early; a backyard rink craftsman can start shaping a clean sheet of outdoor ice as soon as October, and that sheet has the potential to last through March. It was there on the pristine outdoor ice of Virginia, Minnesota, that the brothers first learned how to play and hit and work, and, yes, fight like hell for everything they got.

"Tell me about your local rink where you learned to play," I ask.

"It's funny that you mention that, because there was a great local rink in Virginia," Carlson says. He sits up, leans his thick, muscled frame in, and thumps his tombstone hands on the table. All the attention in the room is pulled toward him with the force of a black hole. "My dad and some other guys ended up getting all the wood, all the fiberglass, and the boards. There was this certain chemical we had that we used to bend the boards to make all the corners. We had the lights, too, and painted all the lines."

Mr. Carlson got a tank from one of the mines where he worked and attached a bar on the back with a nozzle. They'd drive the tank over to the indoor hockey rink, appropriately named the Miners Memorial Building, and fill it with hot water. Then they attached a rug to the back and pulled it around the rink, smoothing out the fresh water that was being put down.

"It was perfect! It would make a perfect sheet of outdoor ice! It was just fabulous!" Carlson belts out. "It was a public rink. But we swept it with brooms and flooded it. We'd tell kids that they couldn't play on it because they didn't do any work. They'd scream and yell, 'But it's not your rink!' Then I'd say, 'Well, it is tonight.' Who's going to argue with that? Who's going to argue with us? *Hahahaha who-ha.*"

It was more than just a sweet sheet of ice, though. For Jack Carlson and his brothers and their father, it was a way of life. It was something that brought them together and kept them together. They were skating all the time, day after day, month after month, always together and on the same line. That's all they did. The community recognized the brothers' connection, too. The guy who ran the indoor rink in Virginia would call their dad and tell him he'd secretly open the rink up just for them on Sunday mornings. He'd just open the back door at seven in the morning, and they could skate till noon. So that's what they did.

"Basically, Steve was the most skilled, Jeff was the toughest, and I was somewhere in between," Carlson says.

The brothers had a natural on-ice chemistry and a shared dream of playing professional hockey together. Always together. After several years playing amateur hockey in northern Minnesota, Jack, Jeff, and Steve got their first tryout in professional hockey as a line.

"We wanted to play in the USHL, and we got a tryout in Waterloo, Iowa. We go down there. It's a two-day scrimmage. There are eleven goals scored in the two days. We're playing on one line and we have eight of the eleven goals."

But, just like in Hollywood, sometimes even a great performance, a great look, or great stats won't land you the gig. The Carlson Brothers' hockey dreams didn't immediately come true, and that reality came with a heavy dose of others' judgment.

"We got called in to the management office," Carlson says. "The manager says, 'You guys aren't good enough to play in the USHL. We can't use you.'"

Of course, the Waterloo manager wasn't the only one to fail to see their gifts right away. One of the greatest insults the Carlson Brothers ever received came years later, from John Mariucci, the legendary Minnesota Golden Gophers coach and State of Hockey icon. "One time, the three of us had a tryout with Mariucci," Carlson says. "He said they only wanted me. But we played as a line and wanted to stay together as a line and told him as much, because, you know, we're brothers. Mariucci said, 'Take your clown act somewhere else, then.' *Clown act*, he said. I said, 'Okay. We will.'"

Unbowed, the Carlson Brothers moved on from their Waterloo, Iowa, tryout and landed another tryout, another audition, and this time they got the gig.

"We played for the Marquette Iron Rangers in Marquette, Michigan, which was also in the USHL." Carlson's smile of vengeance grows large. "The year that we got cut in Waterloo, we played for Marquette. I was voted MVP. I scored 42 goals and had 175 penalty minutes in 55 games. Steve was the center and had 79 points. Jeff was right wing and had 70 points and 170 penalty minutes in 55 games. But Barzee said we weren't good enough. Okay."

His hand goes up and comes down in excitement. *Thump*.

Now Carlson is really rolling, his laughter and his memory bowling along and there's nothing than can stop them. "When we were in Marquette, we played a hockey game inside the state prison. Oh boy, was that scary. It was inside the prison yard. So, Todd, we got eighteen players, and we'd go through a set of doors and . . . *clang*! A door would close behind you. Then a door would open in front of you. Then . . . *clang*! The door behind you would shut. We went through five sets of doors like that inside the state prison to play a hockey game. Holy buckets. Then the prison officers tell us we can't look at the prisoners. They tell us we can't even speak to them. But it was a normal game. The fans were yelling and screaming. It was a treat for them."

Next, the Minnesota Fighting Saints of the WHL held an open tryout, for publicity reasons more than as a source for future talent. That changed, though, when the Carlson Brothers stepped onto the ice and nearly tore the boards down as a three-man wrecking crew. All three brothers were signed and sent as a line to the Saints' minor-league affiliate in Johnstown, Pennsylvania. That town would become the inspiration for the fictional steel city that the Charlestown Chiefs play in in *Slap Shot*.

The brothers took their glorious opportunity to play professional hockey together and skated with it—and, well, *through* it. They felt comfortable playing in Johnstown because it was a steel town. Then Bethlehem Steel shut down and the town became primarily a mining community, just like their hometown of Virginia, Minnesota. It was blue-collar, smokestacks filling the horizon, and the people worked really hard just to scratch out a living. They'd come to the games, drink some beer, and have a good time, and the Carlson Brothers were more than happy to put on a show for Johnny Paycheck.

"Our time in Johnstown playing for the Jets was fabulous. The living arrangements were so nice. All three of us lived together in the same place!" Carlson relates with excitement. "I can always say that my teammates always had my back. But when you're playing with your brothers, it's awesome. I mean, I didn't even have to yell on the ice. I knew exactly where they were. If one was going to dump it in, I knew it. We'd just cycle the puck and cycle the puck. The communication between us was so great."

The Johnstown team hadn't had a lot of success in years past. Then these three showed up and started winning some games, and the Jets ended up winning the championship that year. The Carlson Brothers proved they belonged. They contributed to the team in both points and penalty minutes and were renowned for sticking up for each other. Just like when they were kids, each brother played his role: Steve led the team in points, Jeff was a penalty-minute leader, and Jack had 27 goals and 250 penalty minutes in only 50 games. Jack eventually got called up to the Minnesota Fighting Saints and never returned to the minor leagues.

Although Jack Carlson never got screen time in *Slap Shot*, since he had been called up to play actual professional hockey at the time of filming, the wild, real-life on-ice anarchy with his brothers inspired screenwriters to craft some classic scenes. After Carlson got called up to play in the pro, a tough guy named Dave Hanson moved into Jack's role alongside Jeff and Steve, and the characters were renamed and became the Hanson Brothers. The character of Dave "Killer" Carlson was based on Jack Carlson's real-life on-ice persona.

Most of the mayhem and hilarity involving the trio in the movie is drawn from the real lives of the brothers. One example is the character of Ogie Ogilthorpe, the psychotic goon with a mushroom cloud Afro who features prominently in the last scenes. Ogilthorpe was not just a legendary villain created for cinematic drama, though. He was a real man and a real menace, one whom Jack Carlson dealt with directly.

"Before I went to the Fighting Saints, I played for the Minneapolis Junior Bruins. We were in a league with Thunder Bay," Carlson explains. "We had all heard about Bill Goldthorpe, the man that inspired Ogie Ogilthorpe from *Slap Shot*. Goldthorpe couldn't come to the games because he had just gotten out of prison or something and they wouldn't let him into the country."

But, just as the events in the movie unfolded, the Carlson Brothers eventually came face-to-face with the legend they kept hearing about.

"They finally came down to play us. But we had a tough team. Me and my brother Jeff and Jim Boo. We played them and Goldthorpe, and it wasn't even close. They got their asses handed to them. You always heard about guys like Goldthorpe. He was a yapper. During the games you'd hear these guys like him yapping away, and I would look at them and say, 'Really?' I'd look at them as they were yapping and say, 'Really? You're talking? Really?' The talkers like that never bothered me. It was the guys that didn't talk that were the ones that scared me. The quiet ones would surprise you."

Then there was the centerpiece scene of *Slap Shot*, when the Hanson Brothers start an all-out riot by going into the stands to fight some fans after one of them climbs the glass and throws a keychain, hitting one of the Hanson Brothers in the head.

That cinematic moment was, in fact, a major part of Jack Carlson's actual family history on ice. The Carlson Brothers weren't following any script or directorial instructions, though. There were no Hollywood producers or motor-mouth agents involved. The Carlson Brothers were just being brothers.

"We were sticking up for each other," Carlson says. "Well, in reality, we were in Utica, New York. We're at a face-off, and a guy comes over the top of the glass and throws a rolled-up program at Jeff, and it hits Jeff right in the head," Carlson says. "My brother Jeff was really, really tough. Jeff climbed the boards and jumped over the glass and goes after the guy. I looked over and saw my brother going up and over the boards and the glass, and, you know, it's my brother, so I was right behind him, and I'm going over the glass, too. We got into the stands and got into some fistfights in the stands with some fans."

"We got arrested. We were charged with fifth-degree assault. We went to jail after the game and were there for the whole weekend!"

There was no hilarity in jail, though, unlike in the movie, in which the Hanson Brothers call a massage parlor and order a pizza with their one phone call. Even in the rough-and-tumble world of professional hockey in the 1970s, beating people up in the stands was over the line.

Carlson's really laughing now, really rolling, at the shenanigans that made him and his two brothers so popular in film and on the ice. "But we're hockey players. So, we just think this will all pass over. . . . At the end of the season, we had to go back to Utica, New York, that summer and stand in front of a judge. The judge just reams us a new one. He's saying all sorts of stuff—'These people paid good money, and you're beating them up! What are you guys doing?!' The judge gives us a five-hundred-dollar fine and a year probation. Todd, that summer we had to meet with a parole office over in St. Paul, Minnesota, once a month!"

The legal fallout was far from over, however.

"It stayed on our records, too. Twenty years later, I'm doing some ice fishing in northern Minnesota. Then we head out of the boundary waters and into Canada. I call the Fort Francis Station and they say, 'Uh, Mr. Carlson, have you ever been arrested?' I say no. Then they say, 'Um, yeah, you have. What's this about Utica, New York? What happened in Utica? You have fifth-degree assault charges from there.' This was twenty years later!"

The hilarity, the violence, and his reputation as one of hockey's toughest fighters would eventually allow Jack Carlson entrance into the elite ranks of the NHL. After his rampaging stint with the Minnesota Fighting Saints and the New England Whalers in the World Hockey Association (WHA), Carlson joined the Minnesota North Stars and assumed his familiar role. He was added to the Minnesota roster solely because his hockey heart was as stout as any in the league. Carlson never backed down.

"People always ask me how many fights I won and lost," Carlson says. "I don't know. But I do know that I showed up for every one of them! *Hahahaha who-ha!*"

Before Carlson was traded to the North Stars, the team had suffered through a brazen act of arrogance and petulance by the Boston Bruins, and Carlson was brought in to transplant a healthy hockey heart back into the lineup.

During the 1970s and early '80s, there was a history between the Minnesota North Stars and the Boston Bruins, a history that wasn't kind to the Stars. The Bruins had garnered the reputation as one of the biggest and nastiest teams in the league, and they bullied the Stars unmercifully at every turn. Since their inception in 1967, Minnesota had cowered when playing in Boston and had never won a single game in Boston Garden. Not one.

Worse than the losing, though, was the Bruins' sneering dismissal of the entire Minnesota franchise. In 1977 this took the form of Bruins enforcer John Wensink, whose actions during a game between the Stars and the Bruins would live in NHL infamy. Immediately after Wensink pummeled the North Stars' Alex Pirus in a one-sided fight, he skated over to the Minnesota bench and challenged the entire team. Wensink, a hard man with a giant head of hair and a handlebar mustache, stood right in front of the whole Minnesota team and motioned the entire team to come out and fight—that he welcomed any other challengers. No one on the Minnesota bench moved. No one budged.

Glen Sonmor, the combative Minnesota North Stars coach, was standing behind the bench when it happened, and he felt his team's spine go as limp as wet spaghetti. Wensink gave the team and its coaches and the entire franchise a disgusted hand wave, motioning them to just leave; just get out and let the adults play.

A short time later, Sonmor acquired Carlson in an attempt to inject strength back into his franchise and guarantee that their hockey heart would never be humiliated again.

"A couple seasons before, Wensink challenged the Stars," Carlson recalls. "Challenged the whole bench, and no one reacted. I wasn't on the team then. I was in Hartford. They traded for me the next year. Glen loved the guys that were there to stand up for the team. He loved the skill guys, too. But he molded his team that way. To stand up. I think Sonmor was one of those guys that if you got challenged, you better react."

On February 26, 1981, the line in the sand was drawn. Sonmor and the North Stars decided that they had had enough.

Steve Payne, the North Stars' elite forward, put it this way: "Glen was thinking, The hell with this. We have to put an end to this stuff. Here and now. Let's make a stand and make the statement: If we come into your building, let's play hockey. If you don't want to play hockey, that's fine. We can fight. One way or another, we're not taking your crap anymore."

Sonmor even made an official declaration of war to his boss, Lou Nanne, the North Stars' general manager. "Glen was a tough player and a tough coach," Nanne recalls. "When we played Boston, we knew we were going to play them in the playoffs. Going into Boston on that last game, it was the last time we were going to see them before the playoffs. We'd never won in Boston. Glen called me up and said, 'Louie, I think we should make a stand tonight. We might not win the game. But we're going to fight every one they have on their team. We're going to show them we're not going to back down from them.'"

Sonmor entered the visitors' dressing room in Boston Garden and told his team that this was the night the bullying stopped. The North Stars were more than likely going to face the Boston Bruins in the NHL playoffs in a matter of weeks. Now was the time to cut the shit and stand up for themselves. Carlson was there and ready for the fight at hand.

"Before the game, Glen said we are going to turn the faucet on tonight and we're not going to shut it off." Carlson smiles at the memory. "We're going to dictate the night."

Minnesota's line in the sand resulted in 392 penalty minutes in one game—a record-breaking fight night that involved 67 penalties in the first period, 16 majors, and 13 game misconducts.

The fights started less than a second into the first period and didn't stop until there weren't any more players to fight. There were line brawls and so many players thrown out that at one point there were only six players on each bench. Oh, and there was the incident in the hallway when a cameraman was attacked.

At the opening face-off, North Star Bobby Smith, a true NHL dove, dropped the gloves at .7 seconds against Boston's chippy, mouthy Steve Kasper. With eleven minutes left in the first period, a line brawl erupted, and everyone on the ice was engaged. Payne got into a heated fight, and after it was broken up he took an extra swing and nearly hit the referee, which earned him twenty penalty minutes. Carlson took on Terry O'Reilly because he was the toughest man Boston could offer, and after several other altercations was soon tossed from the game. When Minnesota's Craig Hartsburg and Gordie Roberts were being ejected, the Boston Garden practically blew up. The exit tunnel was conveniently located adjacent to the Bruins' bench, which allowed for intimate interaction with the home team and their fans. As Hartsburg and Roberts were being thrown out of the game, they got into it with the riled-up Boston fans.

"Hartsburg and Gordie Roberts were getting escorted off the ice, and that's when all hell broke loose," Carlson says. "The fans could reach right over and grab your helmet if they wanted to. And they did. The exit tunnel went right through Boston's bench. They changed the arena after that night."

As Hartsburg and Roberts fought with the Boston fans, the Bruins players came to their fans' defense, and soon a massive scrum developed inside the tight quarters of the tunnel. A log-jam of angry players and police and security guards and NHL officials formed. Even the arena cameraman was attacked. And the fights continued from there.

"That was Glen's motivation behind doing what we did. It was all premeditated. It was all very deliberate," Payne says. "Our mission that night was basically to kick the shit out of the guy next to you until he gave up. That's all we cared about."

The penalty boxes were so overcrowded that the NHL game officials who typically sat in there during the games had to move out. The second period started two hours after the game began, and seven North Stars and five Bruins had already been ejected.

"After you got tossed out and you showered, you had to stand in an area inside the arena. We couldn't mingle with anyone. It was closed off," Carlson says. "We all knew what the East Coast crowds were about, especially in Boston and New York. So we stood in the stands in this little spot surrounded by police."

The North Stars lost the game 5–1, but that was beside the point. In fact, Minnesota hardly bothered looking at the scoreboard.

"After the game, Sonmor came into the locker room and said, 'All right! Mission accomplished, guys. But I got one question: Who the hell scored the goal?'" Payne remembers. "We didn't care about scoring any goals that night."

Sonmor was the happiest guy in the world. He was grinning ear to ear, because the fights brought camaraderie. The Wensink incident would always be remembered, but the

North Stars had officially moved past it, because all the players had finally stuck together. This sort of solidarity was right in Jack Carlson's wheelhouse. He loved that in his family and in his hockey teams, and that's why his hockey heart was so valued in the hockey community. His ethos started way back in Virginia, Minnesota, when the Carlson Brothers learned to play the game any way their opponents wanted it.

"I'd line up against Terry O' Reilly or Stan Jonathan and I'd ask them, 'How do you want to play it tonight? Because we're ready. We'll play it anyway you want it,'" Carlson tells me. "Their reaction was like, 'Holy crap.' One of the things Boston didn't realize was that we were a tough team. We had myself, Brad Maxwell, Gordie Roberts, Greg Smith was tough as nails, and Al MacAdam was one of the toughest players I ever saw. Steve Payne was a big, strong kid, too. We were an extremely tough team. We just didn't play that way."

The game was so heated that even the coaches got into it. Sonmor tried to fight Boston coach Gerry Cheevers, because he figured he got his guys into it and he had to do the right thing and get into it, too.

Minnesota's all-out commitment to the fight and to healing their hockey heart on that fateful night was so strong that it extended way past the confines of the ice rink. Not only did Minnesota need a police escort after the game—the team bus had to drive inside the arena so the team could safely load up and exit the grounds—but the message Minnesota sent that night is still heeded today.

"The end results were a month later, we played Boston in the playoffs in the first round and we swept them," Payne says. "They had home ice advantage, too. We swept them right out of the playoffs. They didn't want any more of that with us. Since then, the Minnesota franchise has never had a problem playing in Boston."

BUT FOR CARLSON, HIS career wasn't *all* about the fights and bedlam. Underneath his role as enforcer was a certain childlike enthusiasm. On the ice, he was one of the toughest players the sport had ever seen. Off the ice, though, he was a complete wild card, a goofball who loved a good laugh as much as he loved a good scrap.

"What's the funniest thing you've ever been a part of in hockey?" I ask the jolly giant.

He rears back in his chair, eyes bulging out, and howls with a glorious, glowing memory of Glen Sonmor and his particular artificial appendage.

During the national anthem before a game, teammate Greg Smith and Coach Sonmor were disappearing down below the boards and popping back up. They were turning around, scrambling about, and obviously looking for something. Both of them were popping up and down like a couple of prairie dogs. At the end of the song, Carlson found out why.

"I'm standing on the bench during the national anthem, and Greg Smith finally nudges me," Carlson says. "He says,

'Hey, Jack. Glen's looking at you.' Then I look all around for Glen and see nothing. Then I look down, and there's Glen's fake eye on the ground, and it's turned over and staring right at me."

Carlson loved a good prank, too, and he did not discriminate in his targets. He had the willingness to take on every fighter in the league, so it was only natural that he'd have the stones to go after hockey's greatest player of all time, too.

"Gordie Howe loved to goof around, and I just messed with him all the time. Me and my teammate Bill Butters just messed with him. Doing pranks on him all the time. We used to put his clothes in water and then put them in the freezer. He'd come back to his locker and his clothes would be hanging there all stiff as a board. At our postgame meals there'd always be ice cream. We'd mound his bowl with butter instead of vanilla ice cream and sprinkle chocolate sauce on it. We'd watch Gordie eat all this butter and just go, 'What the heck,' and he'd laugh and laugh."

But his best prank was yet to come. Carlson and fellow Minnesotan Butters lived together for four years and were up to their elbows in pranks. On a road trip to Quebec City, they were holed up in a hotel room, eighteen floors up. They had obtained little plastic bags for ice and filled them with water and started dropping them out the windows and joyfully listened to them hit—*boom...boom...boom*—on the sidewalk.

"I looked at Billy and said, 'Gosh, what would happen if we got this garbage bag and filled it with water?' So that's what we did. We filled up a garbage bag with water," says Carlson, his laugh thundering around the coffee shop. "It took both of us to lift it up and throw it out the window. We hit a Volkswagen that was parked below on the street, and when the bag of water hit the car it blew out all the windows. All the windows! Boom! We pulled the shades and locked the door and hid after that one."

As he talks, Carlson looks out at the street and a world that is stirring awake. As the joking subsides, he reflects upon his dreams, on the hockey career he had with his brothers, and their real-life actions in the WHA and the NHL that weaved in so seamlessly with the fiction of a motion picture.

Carlson knows that in sports, just as in Hollywood, talent is often not enough. Not only do you have to work hard but a little bit of luck has to be sprinkled in, too. Carlson feels grateful that his story—the one in which the son of a miner makes it to the world of professional hockey—is immortalized on film, because, most important, the story of the Carlson Brothers is a story about family. It's about three boys who refused to back down, who fought anyone in their way, whether on the ice, in jail, or in the stands. Jack Carlson is to this day amazed by the Hollywood ending.

"How often do you get the chance I got? To be a Minnesota kid, from the Iron Range, and play professional hockey in your home state and get a chance to go to the Stanley Cup Finals? It's pretty nice," Carlson says. "Did the moon and the stars line up for me and my brothers? Yeah, absolutely."

The sound of hissing milk begins to engulf the coffee shop, and our interview comes to a close. As I put away my recorder and notebook I casually mention to Carlson that I'm having a hard time finding pictures of him that I can use for the book.

"Hold on. Stay right here!" Carlson belts, as he turns and strides out the front door. In seconds the front door blasts open and signals his return. Hollywood and hockey dissolve into one as Carlson hands me three 8x10 head shots from his playing days. "Here. Take these."

I stare closely at one picture. Carlson is in his dark-green Minnesota North Stars jersey and leans on his stick in a classic hockey pose. And then I see it: a large, fresh scar, red and raw, right next to his left eye, from the time in Philadelphia when he took a skate blade to the face that almost blinded him. It is not a blemish made in a costume department. There are no special effects here, because Jack Carlson earned that scar the hard way. He is not a Method actor, and he doesn't need to get into character. Carlson doesn't need to learn his lines, and he certainly doesn't need coffee. He sits before me roaring with the deep laugh of a giant. His massive hands go up, do a jive, come down, and hit the table.

Thump, as hard as dumbbells.

CHAPTER EIGHT
ZACH PARISE

The media jackals are out, and they are starving. The Minnesota Wild have been swept in the second round of the 2015 Stanley Cup playoffs by the Chicago Blackhawks, losing to their dreaded conference rival for the third year in a row, and now it is the official last day of the season and of media availability. Packs of Twin Cities reporters arrive at the Wild locker room scrounging for answers now that the dust has settled. Everyone wants to ask the players what the hell happened as they clean out their lockers and pack up their equipment before heading off into the abyss of summer. All the print and television media folks huddle in the hallway just outside the closed locker room doors, ready to pounce as soon as they open. They are eager to pick some last scraps of meat off the carcass of Minnesota's season.

The media scrum grows by the minute, and they are all there: veteran newspapermen slumping along in sensible brown shoes and Dockers, their crumpled flip notebooks in hand, doing old-school, ink journalism for the two newspapers in town; the NHL insiders and Twitter kings sniffing for any crumb of information that they can blast into cyberspace to their legion of followers in a never-ending pursuit of hits and clicks and online shares and faves; the television men spritzed up with Old Spice and blinding-white teeth shining against tans far too dark for a lukewarm Minnesota spring; the camera crews looking for a face and a voice to use on the evening news one last time before all eyes turn toward the Minnesota Twins. There are outliers, too—the online reporters and website wonks who hang on the fringes, not quite in and not quite out, microphones fastened to the ends of long ski poles and held aloft from the back of the pack, getting close enough only to still get their quotes. And then there's me, the admittedly dim-witted journalist working on a book, rummaging around for story lines.

After a few minutes of small talk, the locker room doors swing open and the media hounds spill into the empty Wild locker room and eagerly wait for the public relations depart-ment to furnish a few Wild players. From behind a closed door at the far end of the locker room, a solitary player appears and fights his way through the throng of media to get to his stall. Before the player is even settled at his locker, the pack of report-ers pounce and swarm, the beat writers jockeying with the television crews, the long tentacles of microphones stretching everywhere. The bright lights of the numerous news cameras come alive in an instant, illuminating the player's tight gri-mace. He sits in the harsh and ugly spotlight of defeat.

The scene repeats itself over the course of an hour. One at a time, a Wild players drift out through the doorway, and the media swarms.

After some time, my busted nose leads me away from the pack and toward the far end of the dressing room. I find myself standing at forward Zach Parise's stall. No one pays any attention to it. His nameplate has been removed, but the locker looks exactly like it has all season. The helmet is still mounted in place on the top of the locker; it is a crisp white, and the visor is as immaculate as a church window. The skates hang upside down on hooks, laces slack, the boots open and yawning and waiting for his feet to slide in. The jersey hangs just so.

Off to the side of the stall dangle Parise's shoulder pads. His CCM pads are the same kind his linemate Jason Pominville wears, which are hanging two locker stalls down. But what makes Parise's shoulder pads different from Pominville's and most of his other teammates' is the heavy wear and tear in a specific area. The part of the shoulder pad that hangs over Parise's lower back has been worn through; the layers of foam and cloth and heavy stitching are completely frayed and blown out, a testament to the staggering amount of abuse Parise absorbed over the course of the 2014–15 season as he battled for every square inch of ice, particularly the area in front of the net where opposing defensemen like to perform angry drum solos on his lower back while he screens goalies and looks for tips and deflections.

But the worst pain of all occurred when Parise lost his beloved father, J. P. Parise, in January 2015, a wound that even the vaunted Wild medical staff couldn't heal.

Over the course of his career, Parise has been known for his remarkably high pain threshold, and he is pound-for-pound one of the toughest players in the world. He is an elite talent who has the uncanny ability to absorb every blow his opponents throw at him, blows that have knocked his teeth out, shattered his bones, and cut his flesh. But as he watched his father struggle with cancer and the horrifying treatment that came with it, the emotional pain was unrelenting. In the end, J.P. lost his brave battle, and Zach felt the heavy, saturating grief that comes from losing one's father.

The physical scars and lost teeth and worn-out pads were one thing. They were on the outside, and were easy to recognize and understand. The narrative was clear: there was a blow of force, and it caused damage that required medical attention or for things to get fixed in the equipment room. More important, the scars on his flesh were not signs of weakness but rather of great strength. His visible scars were a sign to the world that he had taken hits and was still standing. The scar on his heart, though, was the wound no one could see, and it tore him apart on the inside. Every grieving process is different and built around its own unique circumstances. What made Parise's so difficult was that his memories of his beloved father, a legendary NHL forward, were triggered continually by the game of hockey itself, a sport they shared, and he had to visit the source of his deepest pain every day in practices and games and road trips. When J.P. was struggling with cancer, Parise would go to the rink, to his place of work, and grieve;

everywhere he looked, memories sprang up, one after another, from the ice, from the locker room, from the stands, until they were as thick as the North Woods.

This was where Zach Parise was for the majority of the 2014–15 season. He endured both severe physical pain (he suffered a gruesome cut across his lip and also lost a tooth and underwent a brutal midgame root canal) and the emotional pain of losing his father. At times, the pain was so intense that Parise could barely bring himself to the rink to do the one thing he's always wanted to do. Parise kept battling, though, just the way he always had, and his strength was a source of inspiration for his team as they charged through the second half of the season. And after a disappointing start, Parise led the team in goals, and the Wild rallied to make the playoffs.

But now there are no more games to play. It is moving-out day. The off-season has arrived. The reporters interview teammates Thomas Vanek, Mikko Koivu, Ryan Suter, Matt Cooke, and goalie Devan Dubnyk in intervals, but then start to sniff the air, openly wondering when Parise will show up so they can ask him what the hell happened.

Then a back door in the Wild locker room creaks open and the reporters perk up. Parise appears out of a side door close to his locker stall. It is a veteran move, because he has to stroll only three feet out of the darkness and he is already in front of his locker, avoiding the mass of reporters entirely. For a few seconds he is draped in the shadows of a restricted area in the locker room, and the horde doesn't see him. But then they pounce, three-deep, with recorders out, and the spotlight of a disappointing season is upon him.

Parise is known for being the ultimate competitor, never giving up, always staying in the fight till the bitter end. The whole world got to see that when he scored one of the biggest goals in American hockey history to tie the Canadians in the final seconds of regulation in the gold medal game at the Winter Olympics in Vancouver in 2010. He followed that up by leading the underdog New Jersey Devils to the Stanley Cup Finals. But today that resolve has dissipated ever so slightly. His disappointment in having to find answers for why his team suffered the same fate in losing once again to the Blackhawks is palpable.

He stands before the media scrum with the sacrifice written all over him: a large, ruddy scar is still prominently visible under his nose; a new tooth is firmly planted in his lower row; and immediately behind him and to his left dangle his battered shoulder pads.

The season is over, and the damage to Zach Parise has been done, and it is permanent.

To UNDERSTAND PARISE'S PAIN you have to first understand the source of his happiness. For Zach Parise, family life was largely centered on the ice rink. Zach's mom was the two-millionth fan to attend a Minnesota North Stars game at the Met Center, and she won the opportunity to go on a road trip to see the Stars play in Boston. During her prize-winning trip she met Minnesota player J. P. Parise, and the rest is history. Sons Zach and Jordan began their lives as rink rats, an affectionate term for kids who spend all their free time at the ice rink. "The first time I skated was at the Met Center," says Parise fondly, referring to the legendary home rink of the North Stars, where his father was a favorite player and coach. "My dad used to take us out onto the ice at the Met Center and taught us how to skate there."

Like a lot of Minnesota fathers and sons, the bond between the Parise men was forged in the frosty confines of the hockey rink. J.P. immersed Zach and Jordan in the vibrant world of hockey from an early age. They spent their time in locker rooms down in the bowels of ancient stadiums, where they ran around unimpeded.

"My dad knew all the security guards," says Parise, smiling. "And they just let us go."

A sheet of ice, a puck, and a net have been Zach Parise's home since the beginning. After J.P. retired from professional hockey as a player, he stayed at the rink working for the Minnesota North Stars, and then became the director of hockey operations at Shattuck–St. Mary's, a prep school in Faribault, Minnesota. J.P. helped Shattuck become a world-renowned hockey incubator, one that produced Jonathan Toews, Sidney Crosby, and countless other NHL and Division I talents.

Zach was right there next to his dad the whole time at Shattuck–St. Mary's, shooting pucks and playing pickup at every turn. Parise was on the ice all day and night and was given special access to the ice rink to satisfy his near-constant jones for puck time. He even learned how to drive the Zamboni so he could always have fresh ice, even late at night.

"When my dad became the director of Faribault," Parise says, "he gave us keys to the ice rink. We were so lucky."

In that hockey cocoon, though, Parise inherited something from his father that was far greater than the keys to the castle. Stemming from his own career in professional and international hockey, which was built on doggedness and sweaty fortitude, J. P. Parise provided his son with an athletic blueprint for his own career in the sport. Although Zach never saw his dad play live, he learned his father's lessons well.

"Zach is just like his dad," says Lou Nanne, one of the godfathers of Minnesota hockey, who was a close friend of J.P.'s. "He's relentless, and he's got J.P.'s work ethic. Same thing. They both work extremely hard, and they're guys you know every second they're out there they will be working."

J.P. was an old-time hockey legend, a gregarious NHL player whose raucous, swashbuckling playing style was beloved by fans and teammates in the 1970s. Zach's balls-out, inexhaustible puck-pursuit style is a replica of his father's, albeit with slightly less mayhem. J.P. was a key member of Team Canada when the Canadians squared off against the mighty Soviet Union in the legendary Summit Series in 1972. Zach inherited his dad's tenacity, which has resulted in a stellar career in the NHL and captaincy of the U.S. men's hockey team at the Winter Olympics in Sochi, Russia, in 2014 (yes, that's right—Zach Parise is literally Captain America).

While Zach's skating, stick handling, and scoring ability is a lot higher than J.P.'s, father and son both share the same core talent. "J.P. was the best cornerman in the league, and Zach is a terrific cornerman, too," says Nanne. "They both have a motor that doesn't stop, and people who go against them know they're going to be hounded and pestered, and it's going to be a battle all night."

Zach Parise's toughness—just like his father's before him—lies in the fact that while he's not the biggest guy on the team, he makes his living by fearlessly going into the corners, in front of the net, and along the boards, all the while knowing he's undersized and he's going to get hit and speared and shoved.

"Fighting is just one part of toughness. Then there are guys like Parise. He's a tough guy. He's not the guy who's going to fight or anything. But he's a tough bastard," says Charlie Coyle. "You see him in the corners, and how hard he works, and he's bumping. He's not a big guy, but he comes out with the puck almost every time. That's tough."

In a testosterone-charged hockey world filled with alpha males, Parise might be a smaller dog, but he has a big bite. Teammate and fellow Olympian Ryan Suter is widely considered to be one of the NHL's top defensemen, and he has battled with Parise his entire amateur and collegiate hockey career, and now is consistently matched up against him in practice.

So Suter has an intimate understanding of how tough Parise actually is.

"The biggest thing about Zach is his tenacity," Suter says. "It doesn't matter how big or small the guy is that he's going up against, he's going to compete. I think that mind-set is his biggest asset." Because of his dedication to training, Parise is now one of the game's toughest players to move off the puck, a fact that belies his somewhat small stature (5'11", 190 pounds). "People talk a lot about his work in small areas, the battles, but it's all in his balance. He's solid. You run into him, and he's not going to get knocked off," Suter says.

Coyle knows exactly why Parise found himself in front of Canada's crease and scored that monumental goal in the Vancouver Olympics. "He hounds the puck," Coyle says. "His work ethic tops everything he does. His work level, his battle level, his competition level is awesome. Clearly he has a lot of skill and great hands, but the way he hustles, he doesn't wait for things to happen. He *makes* them happen."

Parise has scored 475 points (227 goals, 248 assists) in 587 NHL games, with a large percentage of his points scored from the areas around the net. Despite his all-world talent, Parise continually dedicates countless hours before and after practice to working on his hands, specifically with hand-eye coordination exercises around the net.

"He knows that if you're going to score, you have to go to the net," says Coyle. "He's always ready for rebounds, always hounding near the net."

J.P. and son Zach became linked by their shared playing style. But the on-ice connection between the Parise men was only half of the bond. All of the stories they shared or absorbed about the minutiae of the game, about all of the old-time players and strategies, tied them together in a way that went far beyond mere X's and O's. As the Parise boys grew up, hockey became a language in which J.P. and his boys communicated their love.

The connection between Zach and J.P. was so deeply rooted in hockey and the state of Minnesota that after Zach spent seven seasons playing for the New Jersey Devils and led them to the Stanley Cup Finals in 2012, he returned to his home state and signed a blockbuster deal with the Wild. J.P. and Zach quickly settled into the Xcel Energy Center and reinforced their bond.

The blockbuster contract did not alter the habits and principles Parise inherited from his father, though. Parise was still a rink rat, the sort of player who showed up early to the Minnesota Wild's practices to get in extra work tipping pucks, and he stayed late, too, to work on his shooting from in close and around the net. One of the best all-around forwards in the NHL, a player with astonishing offensive skills and leadership, was still, in his hockey heart, a local Minnesota kid, the sort you could always count on to be there at the rink, ready for the game—any game at all—with whoever showed up to play.

And J.P. was right there with him. He came to most of Zach's games and attended practices, too. If he couldn't make it, there would be a phone call afterward to recap and to chat about the game and life and all points in between. That was how J.P. showed his love, by talking to his son about the inner workings of the sport they both shared, the good and the bad, the goals and the misery. J.P. was always there, ready to listen.

But cancer cruelly changed that.

"My dad was the guy I talked to," says Parise. "I talked to him after every game. During this season, toward the end when he couldn't talk or after he died, all of sudden he wasn't there."

The worst of Parise's pain radiated from this void, this silencing of their daily banter where J.P.'s booming voice and laughter once was. Parise was not alone in his grief, either. One of the harshest realities for the bereaved is getting used to our loved ones simply not physically being around anymore. When a person suffers a slow decline from cancer, toward the end when the disease and the treatment eats away at them every day, each treatment becoming harder and harder, each side effect that much more debilitating, their loved ones begin a grieving period even while the person is still alive. We begin to miss them, to prepare ourselves for their departure, all while still able to see them in the flesh.

But after the burial and the memorial, after all the hand-shaking and hugs, after all the stories have been told, when our loved ones are finally buried, the reality of their loss hits home. Their physical absence is felt in day-to-day moments both big and small, such as holidays, birthdays, graduations, weddings—or, in Parise's case, his father watching him score a series-clinching shorthanded goal in Game 6 of the first round of the 2015 playoffs versus the St. Louis Blues to propel the Wild into the second round. It is in little moments, too. In Parise's case, it was a phone number he always called, a vital lifeline that was suddenly nothing more than beeps, then silence.

THE MEDIA JACKALS CROWD around Parise. They press in, recorders out, the hot camera lights warming everything like tanning lamps. Everyone wants to talk about the season that was, to know why the Wild once again lost to the Blackhawks.

"What happened? This year was supposed to be different."

"What do you think you need to beat Chicago?"

"What went wrong?"

"Are you happy with this team?"

"What does management need to add to the roster?"

Parise's eyes dart around the circle and meet the eyes of every questioner. He stares directly at them as he answers their inquiry. As always, Parise is straightforward and honest. "I don't think as a whole we played well enough to beat them," says Parise. "I thought Chicago played really well. They didn't give us much in the offensive zone."

When asked about the season that the Wild had overall, Parise pauses and seems to sigh as he reflects on everything that has gone on with the team, and with himself as a player and a person.

"A lot of ups and downs," says Parise. "Just a little bit of everything, I guess. I think we did go through a lot as a group. A lot of injuries, sicknesses, times where there really wasn't a lot of room for error."

During the trying 2014–15 NHL season, the Minnesota Wild roster suffered a biblical plague of sorts: Ryan Suter's dad, Bob Suter, the 1980 "Miracle on Ice" iron horse of a defenseman, died suddenly of a heart attack when the team was about to start training camp; several players contracted the mumps, a contagious disease that has long been prevented by nationwide immunization; Josh Harding, a talented goalie who was fighting back from multiple sclerosis, was expected to vie for the starting goalie job but got into an argument during a preseason scrimmage; the two other goalies, Darcy Kuemper and Niklas Backstrom, were like sieves; and the roster was at times gutted by a rash of injuries to key players, particularly the team's hottest scorer, Jason Zucker, who was lighting up the league at a record pace but then broke his collarbone.

Things weren't any better for Parise, as he suffered two gruesome injuries. The first came in New York against the Rangers. Parise was in on the forecheck and grinding for the puck behind the net. His teammate Mikko Koivu's stick blade came up and pitchforked Parise straight in the face. He returned to the game minutes later with a gruesome line of stitches that resembled a fuzzy caterpillar crossing the right side of his lip.

After he got stitched up, Parise, of course, didn't want to make a big deal out of it. He simply shrugged off the pain as part of his job. To the veteran leader, playing in pain was no different than paper getting jammed in an office copier or rush-hour traffic. Yeah, it stinks. But what are you going to do?

"It's all hockey players. It's just one of those things," says Parise. "You want to play. You feel like if you can keep going, you keep going. I got hit in the face. That's a part of the game. It happens."

When he returned from the East Coast road trip, Parise had the eight stitches he received in New York taken out because they were too thick, and he had the cut restitched with a thinner thread. The scar is still a ruddy and jagged line that extends from under his right nostril to the top of his lip.

Months later in Edmonton, Parise caught a puck straight in the mouth, which knocked a tooth clean out.

"He picked his own tooth off the ice!" says Erik Haula, a young Minnesota Wild teammate. "He shows what guys have to put on the line. It doesn't matter what happens. Keep battling, keep playing for your teammates."

Parise simply bent over, retrieved the errant tooth, and then underwent a brutal, toe-curling partial root canal between periods; the nerve was yanked out while he was still in his pads. Then he started the second period.

This was expected, though. Parise was following, as always, the blueprint J.P. had laid out for him.

"Those always hurt," said Parise at the time. "Getting the nerve yanked out never feels good. I'm getting kind of used to them. It doesn't matter, though. Those always hurt. It's a part of the sport. You get hit in the face. That's how it is."

Parise may be one of the best forwards in the world, but he routinely takes more punishment than almost anyone in the league. He takes the abuse and shoves it right back in opponents' faces with his hustle and industrious pursuit, and by scoring goals even after they have done everything in their power to stop him. In the game versus Edmonton when Parise got a tooth knocked out, he was seen minutes later, fighting for the puck in the crease. The usual post-whistle scrum broke out, and an Oiler player grabbed him from behind and tugged at his right cheek. Whether it was deliberate or not, it had to hurt.

The very next game, in Calgary, Parise scored a goal right on the doorstep, fighting his way through an angry mob of sticks and arms and legs, and celebrated his tally with his freshly acquired jack-o'-lantern smile. Despite being repeatedly stitched and bloodied, Parise continued to go into the areas of the ice where the danger was highest and score huge goals, each one of them in high-traffic and high-conflict spots.

"Toughness isn't always fighting," says Chris Nilan, a man who amassed more than 3,000 penalty minutes during his career, nearly all earned the hard way in fights and bench-clearing brawls. "Bob Gainey was tough, and he never fought. Mats Naslund was tough and a goal scorer and playmaker. Toughness is going into the corners and going to the net. Getting cross-checked, getting slashed, and keep playing and not fucking packing it in just because you're getting beat up a little bit."

On the ice, Parise could take anything dished his way. He never packed it in. Not once. Off the ice, though, was a different matter entirely. J.P.'s lung cancer began to spread, and his treatment started to take its toll on him, which emotionally bore down on his son.

"I didn't want to come to the rink," says Parise. "So many different things, so many triggers would make me think of him there."

J.P. was at Regions Hospital in downtown St. Paul, Minnesota, near the Wild's home rink. Parise's daily hockey life was bookended with devastating visits to the hospital: Parise would visit his dad before heading off to practice or immediately afterward, sitting with his father as the cancer slowly ate away at the hockey legend.

"He was always on my mind," says Parise. "But there would be certain things. I'd go out for practice and be in a haze. I remember a couple times almost breaking down and start crying on the ice."

This was especially painful because Parise was in the middle of an NHL season when his father passed, and yet he continued to go to the rink. Each practice, each game, was another day to play hockey, and that had always been Zach's dream. But all of the happy hockey memories that Zach had of his father were being obscured by snow.

AFTER THE MEDIA JACKALS get their fill of Parise and the other players—their Twitter feeds pinging in cyberspace with new intel, their notebooks stained with ink and scribbles, their digital reels loaded for the evening news—they move on down the hallway toward the press conference room, where Wild head coach Mike Yeo and general manager Chuck Fletcher await.

As the locker room begins to clear, it's just me and Parise left standing there in front of his locker. Every piece of equipment is in its right place and ready to go. But the sad reality is that there are no more games to play until next season.

The media disperses, and all that is left are Parise and his scars, the ones visible on his lip and chin and mouth, and the ones that are hidden, dug deeply into the crevices of his memory and cut into his heart. Parise is, pound for pound, one of the toughest players in one of the toughest sports. But standing here in front of his locker, he appears to be a smaller, wounded version of the Captain America that fans have come to know and love. Standing here alone, out of his pads and jersey, all of his hockey heroics sidelined for the summer, Parise has been reduced simply to a son who has lost his father, and he is grieving. "My brother and I were talking," Parise tells me, his eyes welling slightly, "and we were saying that we don't know if we'll ever be over it. It's so weird to say that my dad's not here anymore. I don't know if you ever get over it. But you just try. You try to deal with it the best you can."

Before we wrap up our interview, I show him an old photo of his dad from the 1970s when he played with the Minnesota North Stars. J.P., devilishly handsome with a shag of dark hair and a hard, angular nose, is clad in heavy sweats and stands in his skates on a cement floor, holding a wooden stick with a banana curve, a whistle draped around his neck. Next to J.P. in the photo is my father, Gary Smith, who was working as an athletic trainer at the hockey camp.

Parise stares at the picture and smiles. He notices that his father is wearing the old-school hockey gloves that were ridiculously large and as cumbersome as oven mitts. Then Parise laughs, and it is the kind of honest, guttural laugh that can save a man. It is a laugh that means way more than a simple expression of joy, and is instead a much-needed respite from all the pain and darkness he has suffered during the season. Inside his laugh, a tiny window has been opened after the thunderstorm has passed, and Parise realizes, however briefly, that he has survived—and, in the end, everything just might be okay.

"I remember those gloves," says Parise with a chuckle. The redness in his eyes begins to fade. "He kept a few pairs at the house. We still have them. This summer I have to go through all of his old hockey stuff."

As Parise takes one last look at the picture of his dad, a smile opens up wide, the scar on his lip stretches out, the new tooth gleams, and the warmth of a good memory flashes across his face. It's no coincidence that a little bit of healing occurs right there in the locker room of an ice rink, a place where the Parise men have always found solace.

CHAPTER NINE

THE STANLEY CUP PLAYOFFS

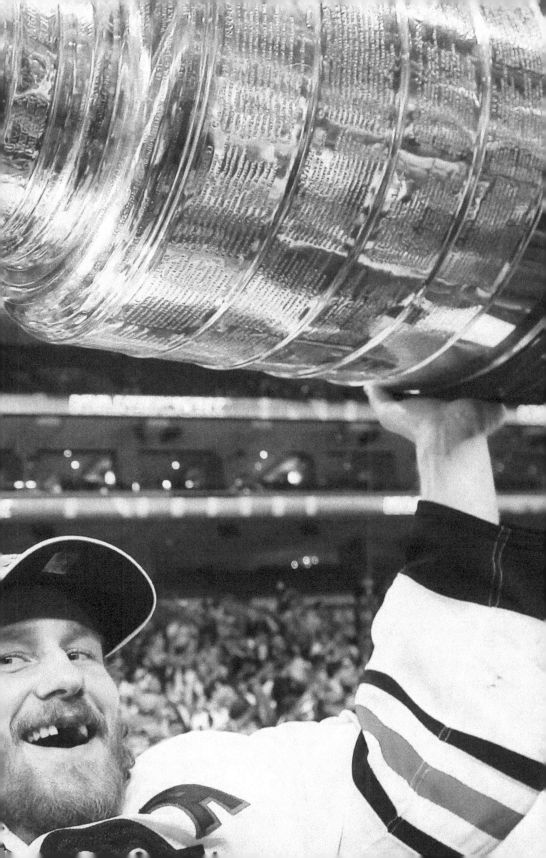

It was Game 7 in the opening round of the 2014 NHL Western Conference Playoffs, the game for all the glory, between the Minnesota Wild and the Colorado Avalanche, and young Wild forward Charlie Coyle wasn't about to sit out just because he took a rising snap shot straight to his face. The shot from the point (from his own teammate Ryan Suter, no less) tagged him square and put a massive dent between his lip and chin. But that didn't really matter all that much to Coyle. He had worked his ass off to get there, left Boston University early to reach his hockey dreams at a faster clip, and spent endless hours training and preparing for the NHL in the minor leagues of New Brunswick, Canada, and Houston, Texas. He had played imaginary Game 7s a hundred times over in the backyard shinny games of his New England youth, too. So he wasn't going to leave the real thing for long just because of a mere flesh wound.

"I knew it was cut but didn't know how bad," says Coyle. "My first thought was, 'Oh, crap, I have to miss a shift. It's Game Seven, and I'm going to mess up the lines!' Then I got back to the bench and the cut exploded."

There were splotches of blood all over his jersey, pants, and skate laces. Once the blood traveled from his face all the way down to his boots, things got serious. The massive and gaping wound still wasn't going to stop Coyle from playing, though. He just headed toward the locker room to get some repairs made.

That's what treatment is called in the NHL playoffs: repairs. When a player gets hurt during the NHL playoffs, the injury becomes less of a medical condition and more of a blue-collar fix-it job. Injuries aren't treated so much as they're worked on, a broken part to be fixed and laboriously put back into working order, no different than a carburetor being taken out, cleaned up, and given a new gasket. When a player is cut or has something broken or something separated during the game, he retreats to the workshop that is disguised as a training room and has his wound hammered, sewn, or bolted shut, mended with tools and tape and glue and needles. Whatever it takes, really, to get it fixed so he can get back out there working again.

A typical NHL medical staff consists of highly educated professionals who have advanced degrees and accreditations from prestigious schools. But during the NHL playoffs, the trainers and doctors become craftsmen, putting players' bodies back together, piece by piece, right there on a bench or in a locker room. They set aside the fancy medical terms, diagnoses, and extensive treatment plans that they learned in school and just start snapping and popping and stitching things back into place.

Occasionally, in the moments when things get extremely heated during playoff games and players don't want to miss a single shift, they'll refuse to leave the bench to receive treatment for their minor cosmetic and dental injuries. So they'll simply spit their teeth out right there on the bench into a gauze pad that has been delicately placed before them by the medical staff.

"They got me right on the table and went to work on it," says Coyle, as if his chin were a clogged fuel filter and not, in fact, a part of his face. Deep inside the Pepsi Center in Denver, Colorado, the Minnesota Wild medical staff performed a quick fix that would have impressed even a Daytona pit crew. "I think I missed six minutes of the period. Right as we were going out for the second period was when they finished putting in the last of the fifteen stitches."

Coyle is a rock-shouldered, big-bodied Bostonian who's got some serious jam in his game. While he's not known for rough play or fighting, he plays extremely hard on the walls and in the corners and bulls his way to the net, often carrying a defenseman on his back. But he's also an earnest, affable guy with an aw-shucks attitude, someone you'd want to marry your sister.

Despite his youthful age (twenty-one) and lack of experience, the importance of the NHL playoffs and the pain you have to endure to win the greatest trophy in all of sports was not lost on him. Even though Coyle was one of the youngest players on the Wild team at the time and had been up with the club for only two seasons, he knew what was expected of him with regard to playing in pain in the NHL playoffs. No coach had to sit him down and give him a history lesson on what the playoffs mean. No veteran player had to pull him aside and give him a heart-to-heart testimonial about how to survive and compete in the NHL playoffs.

All Coyle had to do was look around the locker room. There to his left was Zach Parise, who was battered from his shoulders to his toes from going into every hard area of the ice and battling relentlessly in the crease, taking on every man and shot that came his way despite his short, 5'9" stature. Across the room was Zenon Konopka, a longtime NHL fighter who estimates he's received close to five hundred stitches in his career. Konopka's face looks like a Rand McNally road map. His long journey battling through the minor leagues and the NHL has tattooed his sacrifices onto his skin. His face and hands are full of scars, contours, dents, and markings. Some scars rise and fall, some cut in jagged lines, some even criss-cross each other; some scars are a decade old, while others are brand-new. The old injuries still hurt all the same.

"I've taken two slap shots off my face," says Konopka matter-of-factly. "One was in my first year in Wheeling, West Virginia, when I was playing for the Wheeling Nailers. Shattered my nose. The other time I was playing in Syracuse. That one left this scar on my forehead. Both were from my own guy, when I was in front on the power play."

Konopka pointed toward a scar off center on his forehead that took twenty-seven stitches to close. That old scar on his forehead had remarkably almost connected lines with his latest battle scar, a thirty-stitch cut on the bridge of his nose that he suffered from a wayward high stick from Colorado Avalanche forward Jan Hejda.

"One time I got cut for thirty," says Konopka, not skipping a beat. "They had to put in two layers of stitches. You know when they put in layers of stitches it's usually a pretty good one."

Leading up to the playoffs, Konopka had been playing for long stretches of the season with a broken hand, but continued to fight and take draws. He even took the time to give young Coyle face-off tips.

Standing at the head of the locker room was Wild assistant coach Darryl Sydor, a veteran NHL defenseman who famously got his knee twisted during a game in the 2000 Stanley Cup Finals when he played for the Dallas Stars. Unable to stand up, Sydor crawled and dragged himself across the ice, right back into the goal crease, where he lay down in the line of fire as a human shield for his goalie. There were also a handful of Wild players who were suffering serious injuries but were completely silent about them, choosing not to even acknowledge them publicly and taking their treatment in private.

"There were guys in this locker room who had injuries you didn't even hear about," says Coyle, shaking his head in amazement.

Inside the locker room Coyle learned firsthand that in the NHL, if you want to get the bounty and harvest, you first have to plow the field. It was the same exact lesson learned by

Wayne Gretzky, arguably the best player of all time, decades earlier.

After the grizzled and veteran-heavy defending champion New York Islanders beat an upstart Edmonton Oilers team in the 1982–83 Stanley Cup Finals, Gretzky and teammate Mark Messier walked past the victorious Islanders locker room expecting to see a raging party of popping corks and celebratory bubbly shower. After all, the Islanders had just won their fourth straight Stanley Cup, and that's a helluva reason to throw a party. But when the door cracked open it revealed only beaten Islander players with ice bags draped all over their bodies. Turns out the face of winning in the NHL was not a Wheaties cover shoot. Gretzky and Messier saw that the face of winning was ugly, depleted, and swollen.

Despite everything Gretzky had done that season—setting scoring records every week, every month, putting up 196 points during the regular season (71 goals and 125 assists), 38 points in 16 playoff games, winning the Art Ross Trophy and the Hart Trophy—all of it still wasn't enough to win the Cup. He saw in those ice bags draped over the victors what sacrifice really looked like, and, in turn, rededicated himself to winning the Cup. The importance of playoff hockey was a lesson learned by Gretzky and Coyle (and all manner of players in between) through osmosis, a gradual absorption of what they saw and heard from the players and the stories around them.

"Some players are born with toughness. Some players watch other guys. Some players learn it through experiences," says Coyle.

In Coyle's case, here was a young player, as fresh-faced as a power forward could be in the NHL, and mostly unexposed to the playoff culture. And yet he showed unbelievable character and strength to forge ahead during those 2014 playoffs. At the time he was cut for fifteen stitches, he was already playing with a badly separated shoulder. Worse still, when the Wild won that Game 7 against Colorado, they moved on to the second round and faced the Chicago Blackhawks, in which series he suffered a bad separation in his *other* shoulder. Yes, Charlie Coyle played with two separated shoulders. And despite that, he led the team in hits.

Don't bother making a big deal out of it, though. Coyle brushes it right off.

"It's the playoffs, and everyone is in the same boat. No one is one hundred percent," says Coyle, offering the exact same stock answer that players have given for the last hundred years. "So there really is no excuse. You can't sit around and say that I have this or I have that. I had two separated shoulders. You can't make excuses. It's playoff hockey, and that's what it comes down to."

Forty years earlier, a young Minnesota North Star named Lou Nanne felt the same way. After nearly a four-decade career in collegiate and professional hockey in the state of Minnesota as a player, coach, and general manager, Nanne is now an elder statesman in the Land of Ten Thousand Lakes (and ten thousand ice rinks). Before he took his place in the Mount Rushmore of Minnesota hockey (along with John Mariucci, Herb

Brooks, and Glen Sonmor), Nanne played for the University of Minnesota Golden Gophers and then in the NHL for the North Stars, for whom he battled in the playoffs and suffered a few horrific injuries.

"Every time we played in the NHL playoffs, guys were playing with broken bones and were completely banged up," says Nanne. "We were playing St. Louis in the playoffs and beat them, and then we played Montreal. I cut my elbow really bad. In each game, the cut would open. Then they'd stitch it back up. Next game, I'd cut it again, and they'd stitch it back up. They'd take the stitches out and put them back in."

But that was only half the story.

"After the St. Louis series, we lost to Montreal, and after our playoff series were over I made a USO tour to Vietnam," says Nanne. "I was over there three weeks after the playoffs. I had, like, a tennis ball on the end of my elbow. Every time I'd bend it, pus would squirt out. I came back and went to the doctor and they cut it open. They found out they had stitched part of my elbow pad in the elbow."

As incredible as that may sound, Nanne just rolls with it and has a laugh, because that was simply the way it was during the old-time hockey days of the 1960s and '70s. The equipment was basically cloth. The pads were plastic caps, and they barely worked. When Nanne played at the University of Minnesota, he was speared in the face and fractured a cheekbone. He got some stitches and returned to the game. Afterward, his face swelled up massively and he went to the hospital. The doctor told him he couldn't play, because if he got hit again in the area it would affect his vision.

His Gopher teammates had already left for their next game, at Rensselaer Polytechnic Institute (RPI) in Troy, New York. So Nanne, unbowed by his serious, potentially life-altering injury, had to call the Minnesota head coach, John Mariucci, and ask him if he could still play. Mariucci said sure, as long as he wore a mask. Nanne acquired a lacrosse helmet with a mask that held sponges on his face. During warm-ups, he couldn't see the puck, so he cut out the sponges. The game started and Nanne checked an RPI player, whose hands came up and hit Nanne in the face. Nanne's mask went through Nanne's lip and cut him so badly that he had to get stitches in his mouth. But this kind of thing only prepared Nanne for what was to come in the NHL.

"In Los Angeles, we were playing the Kings," says Nanne, the story breezing out of his memory as easily as a Sunday stroll. "I took a shot in the ankle during the game. We flew to Vancouver the next day. They brought me in for X-rays to see if I had cracked my ankle. The doctor said the ankle was fine. But the X-ray picked something else up. The doctor said the crack in the *other* ankle—my good ankle—was healing perfectly." After a hearty round of laughter, Nanne says nonchalantly, "Everybody in the playoffs went through stuff like that."

All joking aside, though, winning in the NHL playoffs comes down to all the players on the roster gutting it out through both the injuries the know of and the ones they choose to ignore. There are multiple factors that contribute to playoff success, such as timely scoring, rolling four lines, stout defense, and a hot goalie. But the bedrock of all Stanley Cup–winning teams is toughness, mental and physical stamina. The NHL playoffs are a brutal slog unlike any other in sport. A deep run essentially means playing every other night for two months.

"The playoffs are a battle of attrition," says Rick Tocchet, a Stanley Cup winner with the Pittsburgh Penguins who played in pain for the last eight years of his career.

Tocchet was renowned for having one of the highest battle levels in the league. He is the NHL's all-time leader in Gordie Howe hat tricks (a goal, an assist, and a fight in one game) and scored more than 400 points while accumulating over 2,000 penalty minutes. Tocchet knows firsthand that for a team to win the Cup, it needs more than talent and a hot goalie. It needs an absence of memory, the ability to ignore, to forget, to disregard the searing pain that stabs them in the ribs and the throbbing pulse from the broken thumb, and the straight and hard fact that their separated shoulders won't allow them to lift their arms up even to wave for a taxi.

Players win the Cup by mentally focusing on surviving in increments, one treatment at a time, one plodded step out of the training room at a time, one practice at a time, one lap at a time, one day at a time, and one game at a time.

"For two months, the level of play is intense. It's eat, drink, sleep hockey," says Tocchet. "It's the teams that can withstand the soreness and pain and black it out that win. There's the Thursday game, and after the game you're in ice buckets. You have trainers working on you. You probably rest on Friday. Then on Saturday, you do your morning skate to just get back out onto the ice a bit and stretch out. Then at the game you just block it out again. The mental part is just as hard."

It should be noted, too, that all this happens only *after* the players have endured the punishing eighty-four-game regular season, a meat grinder of practices, road trips, divisional rivalries, and games. Still, the NHL playoffs are a whole other level, a period of supreme sacrifice and almost insane intensity.

Along with all the dramatic goals, saves, overtimes, and epic Game 7s in the Stanley Cup playoffs, there is an endless list of stories of players fighting through injury.

"All that lore is carried through," says Chris Nilan, the renowned tough guy who won a Stanley Cup in 1986 with the Montreal Canadiens. "Guys like Bobby Baun playing with a broken ankle and scoring that huge goal. The endless guys getting stitched up, teeth knocked out, and still playing."

Bobby Baun of the Toronto Maple Leafs sustained a broken ankle from a Gordie Howe slap shot in Game 6 of the 1964 finals and returned to the game to score the winner in overtime to even the series. Anaheim Ducks captain Paul Kariya was hit so hard by New Jersey Devils defenseman Scott Stevens in the 2003 finals that he lay motionless and unconscious on the ice for several minutes, until his eyes popped open and his visor fogged over. After a trip to the training room for repairs, he returned to the game and smoked a slap shot for a goal. Chicago Blackhawks goalie Charlie Gardiner won the Cup in 1934 despite suffering from a chronic tonsil infection that had pain eating away at him through the entire playoffs to the point that he died from the infection two months after the playoffs ended. In Game 3 of the 2000 Eastern Conference Finals, Vermont-born moose John LeClair was hit in the face by New Jersey Devils goalie Martin Brodeur's stick, which required a Frankenstein-like thirty-six stitches and caused gruesome black-and-green bruises. LeClair slapped a visor on his helmet and returned to the game. In 1987, the Flyers played the Edmonton Oilers, and early in the series, Philly's Mark Howe got kneed in the thigh, which resulted in a brutal charley horse. At night, Howe slept with his leg tied so it would not straighten out and tighten up. In 1985, Dave Poulin played with three broken ribs for an entire playoff series; the staff had to inject him continuously to try to take away the pain. And then there's legendary Montreal Canadiens forward Maurice "Rocket" Richard, who in 1952, during Game 7 of the Stanley Cup semifinals, returned to the game mere minutes after being knocked unconscious with a bandage covering his forehead and a jersey stained with blood, then skated end-to-end into hockey immortality when he rushed the puck from his own zone and danced through the entire Boston Bruins team to score the series-deciding goal.

"Everyone knows the stories of guys like Kris Draper and Patrice Bergeron [more on that below]. You see what they fought through to win the Cup," says Coyle. "You watch those guys when you're younger and you hear about their injuries. You watch them, and they still go out there and play. Guys set that example."

Every spring more bruises and scars and stories are added to the hockey annals when teams are bounced from the play-offs and finally reveal the true nature of their players' injuries. At that point the team can dispense with the hazy term "upper-body injury," which could mean anything from a player's belly button to his skull.

After the Boston Bruins lost to the Chicago Blackhawks in the 2013 Stanley Cup Finals, it was revealed that Patrice Bergeron of the Bruins did not merely have an "upper-body injury" but had in fact suffered a calamitous number of injuries, unprecedented in the history of playoff carnage. Bergeron is an all-world defensive centerman, a gold-medal winner for Team Canada, and a Stanley Cup winner, and is widely considered to be the best two-way forward in the game. His role is to go head-to-head against the opponent's top forwards at every spot on the ice: penalty kill, power play, face-offs, and offensive and defensive zone coverage. But Bergeron's game isn't predicated on violence, on slashing and hitting and fighting, the style typical of defensive forwards; it's more cerebral than that. Bergeron kills them cleanly with skill, strategy, and a high hockey IQ , a chess master instead of a simple checker. He makes life miserable for the NHL's top forwards by reading the plays in the offensive and defensive areas and taking away scoring chances with precise positioning. Bergeron plays hard in all three zones, and because of it his body has been picked apart, piece by piece, like the guy in Operation.

By the time the Bruins had clawed their way to the 2013 finals, Bergeron had to exert Herculean effort just to put on his pads, let alone play in the games. But in his eyes, it was the least he could do for his team and his city, which had been suffering from the Boston Marathon tragedy of that April.

Oftentimes, sporting events and teams can reflect the mood of a city or a nation (the "Miracle on Ice" is of course a historic example). Athletes and teams can inspire, unite, and rally a populace during deeply charged and emotional times, representing more than just their own team colors. Patrice Bergeron and the 2013 Bruins were all about sacrifice, because the city of Boston, a town built by patriots, has a long and proud history of standing tough. As David Ortiz told the fans at Fenway Park just days after the attack, the terrorists had messed with the wrong city.

In his first few games in the opening round of the playoffs, Bergeron took stitches in his eyebrows and acquired a huge cut across his nose from a heated altercation with Pittsburgh forward Evgeni Malkin. In the postgame press conference, Bergeron wore a camouflage Army Ranger jacket with the Bruins logo on the side, a tradition started by a few of the Bruins' players who were friends with real Army Rangers. It was meant to represent the sacrifices of the military and a warrior spirit and was worn after each game by the player who best exemplified these traits. There is no real way to compare actual combat to a sports game, to compare a real battle to a sports rivalry, to replace a shattered limb or fully repair a life that has been blown apart by a terrorist bombing with a silly game of hockey. The Bruins knew this. But Bergeron was going to give everything he had to try to win the Cup for his team, and, more important, his suffering city, so that they could at least have one moment of reprieve.

In Game 3 of the Stanley Cup Finals, cartilage in his ribs was torn by an awkward hit, and this produced an intense stabbing pain in his abdomen. It hurt to skate, to twist, to turn. To do anything with his core sent waves of pain reverberating throughout his body. He kept moving forward, pushing beyond the wall of his own pain tolerance, because it was the playoffs. Then in Game 4 he broke a rib and had a hard time breathing. But with the emotions of an entire city on his back, the first responders and heroes of the Boston Marathon bombings in attendance, waving their flags in the crowd, singing the rousing national anthem, Bergeron rallied through his building pain.

In Game 5 he took a solid hit that buckled him over in pain, and he nearly went down for the count. But, of course, he played on. At this point the Bruins' medical staff were worried about his spleen and removed him from the game. He kept telling the trainers that he could play through it, but they sent him to the hospital anyway.

The Bruins were down three games to two to the Blackhawks, and the Cup was on the line. Game 6 approached, and everyone was looking to see what Bergeron would do; he felt the desperate need to play. So he saw a specialist, who said the only way he could play was to have a nerve-blocking injection around the area of the cracked rib. He got one that day, and then another on the day of the game. Not feeling quite right during warm-ups, he received another shot. Game 6 started and Bergeron separated his shoulder in the first period, adding to the misery.

By the third period he could barely breathe. The Bruins eventually ended up losing Game 6 and the Cup. After the crushing loss to the Chicago Blackhawks, Bergeron, full of disappointment, headed to Massachusetts General Hospital. A day later it was revealed that in addition to the massive cut on his nose, torn cartilage in his abdomen, broken rib, and separated shoulder, Bergeron was also playing with a collapsed lung.

He was *playing* hockey—in the Stanley Cup Finals—with a collapsed lung.

Even after enduring all of that, Bergeron still remarkably finished the playoffs with 15 points in 22 games. He was such a physical wreck after the postseason ended that during the summer when he got married, he could only honeymoon at his in-laws' cottage in Quebec because he had to undergo such extensive rehab.

Even given all that, in that same season, during those same exact playoffs, on that same exact Boston Bruins team, in that same shattered city, Bergeron's teammate Gregory Campbell nearly trumped him in the pain department. It was during the grudge match versus the Pittsburgh Penguins, and Campbell, a hard-nosed, workingman's player, was guarding the point on a Bruins penalty kill. Penguins forward Evgeni Malkin, one of the hardest-shooting players in the league, ripped a screaming shot from the point. Campbell flung his entire body onto the ice in an attempt to block the shot. The slap shot hit Campbell right in the leg and broke it instantly. But hockey doesn't stop just because a bone breaks, and the game continued.

The Penguins buzzed around the offensive zone trying to set up another scoring opportunity, and Campbell was left stranded out there for more than forty grueling seconds, trying to compete on his broken leg. Grimacing in sheer agony, he used his stick as a crutch and staggered to his skates. He dropped a single glove to the ice almost as a white flag. He couldn't skate and could only move one leg. So he just pivoted in one spot on his one good leg, turning this way and that, trying to poke his stick out for a deflection. The puck mercifully cleared the zone, and Campbell scooted over to the Bruins bench, where he collapsed into the arms of the training staff.

On the other side of the ice during those same exact 2013 Cup finals, the Chicago Blackhawks were equally battered. While Bergeron and Campbell soldiered through their injuries, several of the Blackhawks were playing through their own playoff misery. Bryan Bickell, a rough-hewn NHL power forward, was playing through a grade-two knee sprain that usually required four weeks of rehabilitation, and at times he could barely pick himself off the ice. In a memorable hit in the Western Conference Semifinals, Bickell was absolutely lit up, taken right off his skates in the corner by Red Wings defenseman Jonathan Ericsson, no small feat considering Bickell is 6'4" and 250 pounds. When he stood up, his leg gave out and he wobbled backward, falling down to the ice like a drunken sailor. He gathered himself and tried to stand up again, only to have the leg give out a second time; he wobbled some more and fell straight back down onto all fours. But he played on and fought through the playoffs and the Red Wings and the Los Angeles Kings, because he knew his ultimate role in the Cup finals was to take on Zdeno Chara, the Bruins' 6'9" Loch Ness monster of a defenseman. He did that honorably, too, taking on the Big Z with only one leg. Bickell ended up scoring 17 points in 23 playoff games, including multiple game-winning goals.

Not to be outdone, Bickell's teammate Michal Handzus, the oldest player in the Chicago lineup, played in the finals with a broken wrist and a torn MCL. That fact is ridiculous in and of itself—that a man could steel himself to play professional ice hockey at the highest level in the most intense game with only one arm and one leg at full strength—but it becomes profoundly absurd when you realize that not only did he play but he scored on a shorthanded breakaway in the finals.

While Gregory Campbell holds the ill-gotten trophy for the single most heroic moment in the 2013 finals, Chicago's

Andrew Shaw earned the award for the ugliest. During the Cup-winning Game 6, Shaw, who is affectionately nicknamed "the Mutt," had his own pass intercepted by surly Bruins forward Shawn Thornton, a 6'2" bridge abutment on skates, with a heavy shot. Thornton stole the puck from Shaw, skated over the offensive blue line, and immediately let fly a hard snap shot that Shaw, in an attempt to win back the puck, received full force in the cheek from about two feet away.

The shot hit Shaw so hard from so close that it sent Shaw's whole body into a spiral, twisting him completely around before dropping him to the ice in a blackout. Shaw's stick and one of his gloves flung out and skittered across the ice. He lay motionless on the ice for a few minutes with the Boston fans soundly booing him because, well, it was playoff hockey. Shaw returned the next period with two cuts on his grotesquely swollen right cheek that continuously dripped blood down his face, dressing him in the official war paint of the postseason.

No player in the playoffs is immune to playing in pain. It's a rite not just reserved for defensive centers like Bergeron or third-line grinders like Shaw. All players feel that thread of playoff history tugging deep inside of them, and whether or not they heed it is up to them. From the bottom man on the roster to the captain, if you are in the playoffs, that thread is in there.

It's in a player like Duncan Keith, one of the best defensemen in the world, who has won two gold medals for Team Canada and three Stanley Cups for the Chicago Blackhawks. Keith returned to a decisive playoff game immediately after losing *seven* teeth in one clean shot. Actually, when he lost those seven teeth, he never actually went down, either. He never wavered, never dropped to a knee. Heck, he never even bent over. The opposing team even capitalized on the injury: when the puck hit his face, it took a great bounce that led to a goal. Keith skated off the ice, went in for repairs, and came back out several minutes later and played. He ended up playing over 29 minutes during the game and assisted on the game-tying goal.

"It's just missing teeth," said Keith after the game. "It's a long way from the heart." He didn't die, so he played on.

The unbreakable playoff hockey strength is seen in Rick Tocchet, a hard-charging player who refused to fold physically and mentally. He survived multiple season-ending injuries and fought through them all in his quest to win the Cup. One of his worst injuries was in Pittsburgh, when he was skating on a line with the immortal Mario Lemieux.

"Mario went to dump the puck in and shot the puck," says Tocchet. "It hit me right in the jaw. If there's a guy you want to get hit by, it would be Mario. I didn't mind a broken jaw from him. He got me forty goals with tap-ins!"

Tocchet played through it. He finished the game and even scored the game winner. Then he took four days off. But Tocchet wasn't going out for good. Days after the injury he had a tense meeting with Pittsburgh general manager Craig Patrick.

"They were going to wire my mouth shut. It was going to take three to four weeks," says Tocchet. "I looked at Patrick, and he looked at me. I told him I wasn't going to take a month off. The playoffs were coming. He was leaning toward having me not play for a while. I said that I didn't get traded to Pittsburgh to not win the Cup."

So Tocchet had a protective bar added to his helmet that made him look like a cyborg Abe Lincoln. Days after breaking his jaw, and sporting the new protective bar, Tocchet got into a fight with the Islanders' Kris King in the last game of the season. In round one, Game 1 of the Stanley Cup playoffs versus the Washington Capitals, he fought towering and nasty defenseman Kevin Hatcher. While the fight rallied his team, it incensed head coach Scotty Bowman, because of Tocchet's disregard for his own injury. The Penguins won the Cup, and Tocchet chipped in 19 points in 14 games.

At the center of it all, particularly a team's push through the playoffs, is the team captain. The captain is the thermostat to which the team's mood is set. Over the course of hockey's history, there have been countless examples of a team captain fighting through his own adversity and guiding his team through the playoffs. One prime example is 2002 Detroit Red Wings captain Steve Yzerman, who led his team through the playoffs with sheer will, epitomizing leadership and sacrifice to the point that even his own teammates could not believe it.

In 2002, Yzerman's effort went beyond mere mortal toughness. He was an elite offensive talent, widely regarded as one of the most dynamic players of his generation. But for all his scoring records and highlight-reel goals, inside the locker room Yzerman was known for having a deeper well of pain tolerance than anyone. In 2002, Yzerman led the Red Wings to the Cup while playing on a right knee so ravaged that it would take three surgeries to repair in the off-season.

"Yzerman played on one leg," says Detroit Red Wing Kris Draper. "He would be in a battle and fall down, and he literally would have to use his stick to get back up, put all of his weight on it to help himself get up. He couldn't skate in practice. But not only did he play in the games, he scored huge goals. There were times when he willed us to win."

When Yzerman returned from the 2002 Winter Olympics in Salt Lake City—where he won a gold medal for Team Canada—MRI tests revealed he had almost no cartilage left in his knee. Unbowed, the captain took three treatments a day to mend the knee and get through. He stopped practicing and could barely walk. But he soldiered on and hobbled through his shifts, at times scraping himself off the ice, and yet ended up scoring 23 points in 23 games while taking 23 shots of painkillers to make it through and win the Cup and the Conn Smythe Award for playoff MVP. This was no surprise to Draper or any of the other Red Wings. Yzerman had once suffered herniated disks, near-paralyzing shoulder injuries, and broken bones—and had played through them all. The year before, in 2001, he broke his leg with six games left in the season but refused painkillers and played in Game 1 of the playoffs versus Los Angeles, all the while suffering bone-on-bone scraping.

"We rallied around him and worked harder and harder because we knew what he was going through," says Draper.

Kirk Maltby, Draper's Grind Line teammate on the Red Wings, was inspired to rally through his own injuries after seeing firsthand what his captain was going through.

"To see your captain going out there and blocking shots ... Yzerman would have to use his stick as a cane to get back to his feet," says Maltby. "He was our best player. After the playoffs he had major knee surgery. They basically cut his bone in half to reset it. This was the surgery players get when they're done playing so they can have quality of life afterward. When you see a guy like Stevie doing that, you feel obligated to go out. If it's not broken, it's not hurt."

Twelve years after Yzerman's heroic fight through the knee injury, we saw Maltby's blunt assessment of playing in pain in the Stanley Cup Playoffs fully formed in a young Charlie Coyle. Yzerman's ravaged knee and Coyle's busted shoulders, two generations apart, a first-ballot Canadian-born Hall of Famer and a young upstart from Boston, two stories of agony and unwavering hockey strength, of injury and repair, woven together like the strands of a rope, the thread through time from one player to the next as strong as ever.

"Those stories put you in the mind-set where this guy is doing it, why can't I?" says Coyle. The scar on his chin from that brutal 2014 slap shot was still raw and red nearly a full year after he acquired it, and will remain there forever as the ultimate symbol of sacrifice in the Cup playoffs. "What's different about me? Why should I have to sit out? It's everything on the line."

CONCLUSION

Each interview that I conducted for this book began with the same question: *Why do hockey players routinely play in so much pain?*

I asked current NHL players, NHL alumni, and all manner of hockey personnel. I asked them over the phone, in locker rooms, in the press box, and in coffee shops. With the exception of Jack Carlson, every single player I talked to for *Hockey Strong* had a hard time answering what appeared to be a rather straightforward question.

It wasn't like I was asking the players about global warming and the effects of rising sea levels or their thoughts on the Dickensian narrative of *The Wire*. I was asking them about something they were intimately familiar with, both physically and mentally. But in interview after interview, it was almost as if they had never really considered why hockey players like themselves continuously played in so much pain. Perhaps it is something so commonplace, something that has always been there, like the moon or the presence of oxygen, that they had never given it an ounce of thought. Hockey players play in pain. So has it always been, and so shall it always be. What's there to talk about?

Former Minnesota North Star Steve Payne: "Why do hockey players play in pain? I've never given it any thought."

Former New Jersey Devil Randy McKay: "Ugh, it's just something you do. Wow, that's a tough question. It's hard to explain."

Dave Brown: "I think . . . it's the way it's always been . . . ?"

As each interview moved forward, though, the players would inevitably circle back to that first question in an attempt to answer it. They seemed suddenly just as curious as I was. When each player began to tell his own tales of playing through pain, or when he told stories about a teammate's feats of courage, it was as if he, too, were hearing it and believing it for the first time. The injuries that they sustained in their careers, the ones that they thought were mundane, moments that were completely taken for granted, were discovered to be riveting parts of their narrative. It took some coaxing, sure. All the players interviewed truly believed that their own particular scars or injuries were nothing special, because every hockey player has stories just like them. But they eventually peeled back their layers of stoic pride, the shield that tells hockey players never to draw attention to their own injuries because, in the end, it's all about the team, and winning the Cup as a team. Finally, though, with their willingness to share, my book began to take shape.

As they talked, the stories behind their injuries were unwrapped, revealing years and memories, which led to more stories, more memories, like Russian nesting dolls. After a few moments of flitting around my first question, Payne came around and disclosed to me, "I actually played for seven years with what I would call minor injuries. That's stuff like broken ribs, broken thumbs, broken fingers, and a broken nose." That small observation led directly to him later confessing in our interview that he played three-quarters of his rookie year when he was eighteen years old with a severely broken thumb, which had swelled up to the size of a pickle.

My interview with Randy McKay was also typical. One small story about a minor scar on his chin was a portal to much more.

"Devils coach Jacques Lemaire was the best coach I had in my career by far," said McKay. "When he would get pissed off about someone on the other team, he'd say, 'Give him a fucking whack.' And he said it a lot. 'Give that guy a fucking whack' if someone was out there embarrassing us."

Lemaire assembled the New Jersey Devils' famous Crash Line of McKay, Mike Peluso, and Bobby Holik to handle things on the ice, with a heavy snarl and even heavier fists. With a tap on the shoulder, Lemaire would deploy them to deal with whoever was acting like a fool out there on the other team.

"The Crash Line was something unique, and at the time we were the best fourth line in the NHL. [We'd go into the game] to either keep momentum going or to just get some momentum built," McKay said. "Well, it was a New Year's Eve game in Chicago. My linemate Mike Peluso on the Crash Line, one of the most emotional players that I've ever played with, was forechecking on this one defenseman. At the last second, the defenseman saw Peluso coming and ducked. Peluso went right over the top of him and ended up hitting me instead, right on the side of my face with his skate. I dropped to the ice like a frickin' bag of rocks. Peluso hit me so hard with his skate I got cut on the chin and a concussion, too."

All of the hockey players interviewed for this book gave some version of these general reasons for playing in pain:

- *It was their history and culture.* Almost every player mentioned that the hockey players who played before them all played in pain, and they set the example. So that's what they would do, too. Who were they to break the chain? Who were they to not learn the lessons of their forebears? The thread through time, the one that tied the original players from the 1800s to today's players together, was real, and it was alive.

- *It was a team thing.* Every player I talked to mentioned that they gutted it out because they didn't want to disappoint their teammates. Each one of them knew that in order to be a hockey player, they had to accept the fact that they'd never feel 100 percent, and the injuries were simply going to be a part of their career. The end of the season would feel like hell for all of them, but the team that could win it all was the team that could *endure*. Again, you can't truly compare sports to real warfare. But inside the confines of the hockey locker room, the loyalty the players had for each other was akin to a military band of brothers.

- *It was simply part of their job.* Cody Franson of the Buffalo Sabres said it best: "There's no way to play a season without playing in some pain. When you start to consider this game as a profession, you know you're going to have to play in pain. It's a physical game; you play a lot of games in a short amount of time. I think if you're going to consider hockey as a career, you have to accept that and have a high pain tolerance."

- *The players felt pressure to play in pain.* Most of the NHL alumni that I spoke with told me that they felt like they'd lose their spot in the lineup if they didn't play in pain. They learned quickly that hockey was very much a business just like any other, and if they didn't show up for work, if they couldn't play, they didn't have a job. So they played with an injured foot or hand or shoulder to remain employed. But this pressure to play in pain was also why so many NHL players felt compelled to continue playing despite the lingering effects of concussions. As we've seen in the NFL, chronic traumatic encephalopathy (CTE), a progressive, degenerative brain disease found in athletes with a history of repetitive brain trauma, was lurking in their brains and their very livelihood. For vast numbers of NHL alumni, the research and information on concussions wasn't yet available or completely understood, and the locker room culture was far less forgiving than it is today. So they played through the headaches, the dizzy spells, the depression, the fits of anger, and the metallic buzz ricocheting between their ears, because it was their job to do so, and their teammates were counting on them. The players simply had little idea how corrosive the effect of "having their bell rung" would be for their brains and their futures. Understandably, most of the players that I interviewed didn't want to broach the subject of concussions, either, because it was too personal or because they were involved in lawsuits.

Regardless of their reasons for playing through such staggering amounts of pain, hockey players at every level, from youth hockey to the minor leagues to the NHL, are hockey strong in one way or another. And it is more than just possessing a high pain threshold. Hockey strong is an untouchable and unbreakable spirit that gives the sport its true pulse.

I will leave you with the amazing example of former Dallas Stars forward Rich Peverley.

On March 10, 2014, Peverley suffered a cardiac event during an NHL game and nearly died right there on the bench. It was during the first period of a game between the Stars and the Columbus Blue Jackets, and Peverley came off the ice after finishing his shift (of course he finished his shift) and collapsed on the bench. The game came to a sudden and terrifying halt as Dallas medical personal and EMTs rushed over and carried him straight into the adjacent tunnel, where they administered lifesaving actions. Peverley was given chest compressions, and a defibrillator was used. He was resuscitated just a few feet from the bench.

In the ensuing minutes, as Peverley lay there in his pads, soaked with sweat, he did not speak of angels or of seeing a great, glorious light. He did not come back in a euphoric state of profound love and wonder. Instead, after he regained consciousness, Peverley looked up at Dallas coach Lindy Ruff and had a simple question.

"The first thing he asked me was how much time was left in the first period," said Ruff.

The medical staff loaded Peverley into an ambulance and rushed him to a local hospital. In transport he was alert, and even though his heart had just stopped working and he had almost died and was hooked to oxygen and an IV, he felt as hockey strong as ever.

"I was able to talk to him in the back of the ambulance," said Dr. Gil Salazar, one of the medical staff who saved Peverley's life. "He was able to tell me where he was, and he actually wanted to get back in the game."

Of course he did. Peverley was a hockey player.

A Note on Sources

A great many people were overgenerous in giving freely of their time, energy, and memories, all so I could write this book. The bulk of the material comes from my personal interviews in 2015 with Mike Rupp, Lou Nanne, Charlie Coyle, Zach Parise, Shjon Podein, Paul Ranheim, Dave Brown, Rick Tocchet, Chris Nilan, Randy McKay, Kris Draper, Kirk Maltby, Craig Berube, David Clarkson, Rob McClanahan, Buzz Schneider, Jack Carlson, Steve Payne, Zenon Konopka, Cody Franson, Tom Chorske, and, of course, my father, Gary Smith.

In addition to decades of obsessive hockey watching, I also relied on the journalism and observations of many fine sources, many of which are listed below.

Adelson, Eric. "On His Last Leg, Yzerman Still Leads." *ESPN The Magazine*, June 17, 2002.

Bazelon, Emily. "What Really Happened to Phoebe Prince?" Slate.com, July, 20, 2010.

Buccigross, John. "Buccigross: Blues, Blackhawks and More Podes Than You Can Handle." ESPN.go.com, October 23, 2007.

Cacciola, Dino. "The Brawl." LCShockey.com, April 1, 1997.

Coffey, Wayne. *The Boys of Winter*. New York: Crown, 2005.

Crouse, Karen. "A Delight for Detroit: The Return of the Grind Line." *New York Times*, April 29, 2011.

Cullen, Kevin. "The Untouchable Mean Girls." *Boston Globe*, January 24, 2010.

"Draper Faces Surgery." orlandosentinel.com, May 31, 1996.

Ferris, Lee. "Edmonton—Home of the Hockey Heavyweights." thehockeywriters.com, November 7, 2009.

Feschuk, Dave. "Maple Leafs' Roots Run Deep for Clarkson and Family." thestar.com, October 25, 2013.

Graff, Chad. "Wild's Charlie Coyle Battle-Tested Now, and He Has the Scar to Prove It." TwinCities.com, October 3, 2014.

Grossfeld, Stan. "Chris Nilan Now an Antibullying Advocate." *Boston Globe*, November 25, 2012.

Gwizdala, Mike. "Top 20 Albany Hockey Enforcers." Times union.com, December 24, 2012.

Hayes, Marcus. "Go Forth and Multiply: Put Together to Give Flyers a Rough Time, Grind Line Turning into Offensive Force." Philly.com, June 5, 1997.

Heika, Mike. "Stars Doctors Explain What Happened to Rich Peverley." *Dallas Morning News,* March 10, 2014.

Howard, Johnette. "The Making of a Goon." *National Sports Daily,* February 18, 1990.

Hradek, E. J. "Islanders Show Oilers How Cups Are Won." NHL.com, October 25, 2012.

Irwin, Annette. "Badass Hockey Players." RYOT.org, June 2013.

Kennedy, Kosta. "The Lying Game." SI.com, April 29, 2002.

Kennedy, Ryan. "The Biggest: Bench Brawl." *Hockey News,* November 3, 2013.

Khan, Ansar. "How Kris Draper, the Grind Line, Were Critical to Detroit Red Wings' Stanley Cup teams." MLive, July 27, 2011.

Longley, Rob. "David Clarkson Took Long, Tough Road to Maple Leafs." *Toronto Sun,* September 1, 2013.

Macdonald, Jamie. "Go for the Gold: Zach Parise." USA Hockey.org, February 5, 2013.

Maki, Allan. "The Fight That Changed Hockey." *Globe and Mail,* May 12, 2012.

McCarty, Darren, and Kevin Allen. *My Last Fight.* Chicago: Triumph Books, 2013.

McCoun, Paul. "No Pain, No Gain." BleacherReport.com, January 12, 2010.

McDonald, Joe. "Gregory Campbell Breaks Leg." ESPN.com, June 7, 2013.

———. "Patrice Bergeron Discusses Injuries." ESPNBoston .com, July 2, 2013.

Mifflin, Lawrie. "A Year of Attacks on Hockey Officials." *New York Times*, May 6, 1982.

Muir, Allan. "2014 NHL Playoffs: Injury Revelation Day." SI.com, June 14, 2014.

Pelletier, Joe. "The Hanson Brothers." *Hockey History Blog*, February 21, 2007.

———. "Joe Kocur: K.O. Punch." GreatestHockeyLegends .com, January 9, 2012.

Pennett, Dana. "39 Stitches Won't Keep LeClair Out." Philly .com, May 20, 2000.

Podnieks, Andrew. *The Complete Hockey Dictionary*. Bolton, Ontario: Fenn Publishing Company, 2008.

Powers, Scott. "Handzus Fights Through Pain to Play." ESPN .com, October 4, 2013.

Rosen, Dan. "Keith Loses Teeth, but Shows Plenty of Heart." NHL.com, May 23, 2010.

Russo, Michael. "Parise Family Embraces Life's Good Moments During Tough Times." *Star Tribune*, January 8, 2015.

———. "Parise's Routine with Wild Becomes Far from Routine." *Star Tribune*, January 6, 2015.

Sandor, Steve. *The Battle of Alberta: A Century of Hockey's Greatest Rivalry*. Victoria, British Columbia: Heritage House, 2005.

Souhan, Jim. "J. P. Parise Has Hockey in His Blood and in His Heart." *Star Tribune*, March 28, 2012.

Spector, Mark. "The Battle of Alberta: One of Hockey's Greatest Stories." sportsnet.com, December 23, 2014.

"*Sports Illustrated* Names Xcel Energy Center Top NHL Arena." Wild.com, September 28, 2006.

Steele, Franklin. "The Grind Line." BleacherReport.com, July 26, 2011.

Tanner, James. "Leafs Fans Are Wrong to Say 'Tear It Down'—Should Actually Be Excited." thehockeywriters.com, January 19, 2015.

Traikos, Michael. "Leafs' David Clarkson Sidelined at Least Three Games with Injured Elbow." *National Post,* January 17, 2014.

———. "Toronto Maple Leafs' David Clarkson at Risk of Missing Start of Season for Second Straight Year." *National Post,* September 28, 2014.

Vecsey, George. "Bruins, North Stars Penalty Marks." *New York Times,* February 27, 1981.

Whyno, Stephen. "A Year After Making Maple Leafs Debut, Clarkson Finally Feels Like Himself Again." *Canadian Press,* October 30, 2014.

Wilkinson, Alec. "Examining Joey Kocur's Hand." *New Yorker,* April 24, 1995.

Websites

Brainyquote.com

detroitredwings.com

Flyer Heroes of the Past series, on Flyers.NHL.com

Hockeydb.com

Hockeyfights.com

NHL.com/PlayerStats

Russo Rants, Startribune.com

Films

The Last Gladiators. Alex Gibney. Documentary, Phase 4 Films, September 9, 2011.

Our Tough Guy. Molly Schiot. Short documentary, ESPN Films, *30 for 30* series, November 12, 2014.

24/7 Red Wings/Leafs. Road to the Winter Classic. Documentary, HBO Films, Episode 3.

Radio Programs

Beyond the Pond. KFAN FM, Minneapolis–St. Paul.

"Chris Nilan Talks Boston Roots, Whitey Bulger, Addiction, and Recovery." *Toucher and Rich*, WBZ FM, Boston, January 1, 2014.

Acknowledgments

As I wrote this book, I continued to work at my day job as a laborer for a landscape company in St. Paul. I drove a Bobcat in the summer, a snowplow in the winter, and did various grunt work. Almost on a daily basis, I would punch out at the company time clock, return home, and begin crafting the chapters that would eventually form this book. This dual life as both a blue-collar worker and a writer often left me callused, salty, and hollowed out with exhaustion. But because of the love, support, and collaboration of the following people, my dream of publishing a book became a reality.

First and foremost, I thank my wife, Sarah, because without her love and all-around sass, this book would not exist. Also to my son, Murphy, who is the toughest person I know and continues to be my hero. Gary and Linda Smith, my parents, taught me how to work, how to dig in, and how to take a punch when times get tough. When I was buried in literary rejection, when my daily working-class ache settled deep in my muscles and joints and I wanted to quit, it was your guidance that kept me there at the writing desk, head down and grinding, finishing my shift, and this book is a testament to the work ethic that you instilled in me. A lifetime of thanks is owed to my sister, Becky, and my brother, Tony, for they have dealt with my ignoramus tendencies longer than anyone. A loving shout-out to the Smith kids—Addie, Olivia, and Elliot—for their infectious energy, laughter, and endless soccer games. Also to my wife's family for their support and encouragement over the years.

This book simply would not have happened without my agent, Michael Croy, at Northstar Literary Agency. It was his tireless support and confidence in the book that carried me through the whole process, and I'm immeasurably grateful.

Thanks to Adam Wilson at Gallery Books for his shrewd editorial hand in guiding *Hockey Strong* from start to finish. It was his affable disposition that truly made the process go smoothly. As a first-time author, I can't imagine it having gone any better. Also, I'd like to thank everyone in the art department, production, publicity, and copyediting at Gallery Books and Simon & Schuster who helped with *Hockey Strong*.

Also, endless thanks to the Minnesota Wild and everyone at Wild.com for their help and employment over the years. Specifically, I would like to thank Aaron Sickman and

Carly Peters in the Wild Public Relations Department; Glen Andresen and Mike Doyle, formerly of Wild.com; John Worley, Minnesota Wild athletic trainer; and former Director of Hockey Operations Chris Snow for his encouragement as I took my first steps as a sportswriter. A special thank-you to Zak Brown for the hustle in landing me an interview so long ago.

This project could not have been completed without the cooperation and patience of the following NHL public relations members: Jennifer Bullano (Pittsburgh Penguins), Karen Davis (Columbus Blue Jackets), Zack Hill (Philadelphia Flyers), Mike Kalinowski (Los Angeles Kings), and Steve Keogh (Toronto Maple Leafs). Also, thanks to Jaime Holtz at knucklesnilan.com for her support.

Thanks to my astute editors in the Twin Cities, who have been gracious with their time as I fumbled my way through their magazines and literary world—specifically Chris Clayton and Jon Lurie for believing in me before even I believed in me. Thanks to Ellen Burkhardt, Quinton Skinner, Mo Perry, Chuck Terhark, and Dana Raidt for their friendship. Also, to Aaron Paitich and Reed Richardson at Touchpoint Media for their employment.

For their moral support during this process (and in life), I'd like to thank Thaddeus Morquecho, Matt Simitis, Morris Weintraub, Leif and Heidi Haugen, Nick Brown, Jon Feulner, John McCambridge, Mike Harder, James Quilter, Lorne Petkau, Ann and Steve Prentice, and Jason and Sandri Rutten.

To Chris Pavlich and Jim McGuinn, I thank you for your dude-ness.

A special thanks to Jerome "Pappy" Kern and his sons for helping me balance my life of shovels and scripts.

Finally, a hearty thank-you to all the beer-league hockey players on Team Dudeface, Arden Park, and Todd Park for passing me the puck even though I'm a pylon. Go Dark.

In memory of Joan "Gaga" Feinberg, Jim Bartell, and D. Boon.

Photo Credits

Pages xvi–1: Watched by linesman Bob Luther (right), Canadian professional hockey player John Wensink of the Boston Bruins holds the jersey of, and delivers a right hook to, Wayne Babych of the St. Louis Blues during a game, October 24, 1978. (Photo by Bruce Bennett Studios/Getty Images)

Pages 16–17: Colorado Avalanche Shjon Podein jumps on top of the net to avoid Calgary Flames goalie Mike Vernon after scoring during second-period action in Calgary, Tuesday, Oct. 10, 2000. (AP Photo/Adrian Wyld)

Pages 44–45: Edmonton Oiler Dave Brown (#32) during a fight vs Calgary Flame Jim Kyte (#4) at Northlands Coliseum. Game 3. Edmonton, Canada, 4/8/1991. (Photo by David E. Klutho/*Sports Illustrated*/Getty Images)

Pages 74–75: (L–R) Joe Kocur (#26), Darren McCarty (#25), Kris Draper (#33), and Kirk Maltby (#18) of the Detroit Red Wings Alumni pose for a group photo after their 5–2 loss to the Colorado Avalanche Alumni in the 2016 Coors Light Stadium Series Alumni Game at Coors Field on February 26, 2016, in Denver, Colorado. (Photo by Dave Reginek/NHLI via Getty Images)

Pages 124–25: April 5, 1983: Montreal Canadien Chris Nilan grapples along the boards with the Buffalo Sabre Larry Playfair during the first period of an NHL hockey game in Montreal. (AP Photo/*The Canadian Press*, Bill Grimshaw, File)

Pages 148–49: Buffalo Sabres center Cody McCormick (#8) knocks the helmet off Toronto Maple Leafs center David Clarkson (#71) during a third-period fight in an NHL hockey preseason game, Friday, September 26, 2014, in Buffalo, NY. Toronto won, 6–4. (AP Photo/Gary Wiepert)

Pages 174–75: Rob McClanahan (#24) and goalie Jim Craig (#30) of the USA defend the net during an exhibition game against the Soviet Union on February 9, 1980, at Madison Square Garden in New York, NY. (Photo by B Bennett/Getty Images)

Pages 200–201: 2002 Season: Jack Carlson. (Photo by Bruce Bennett Studios/Getty Images)

Pages 230–31: The Minnesota Wild's Zach Parise (#11) and the Edmonton Oilers' Andrew Ference (#21) mix it up during first-period NHL hockey action in Edmonton, Alberta, on Tuesday, January 27, 2015. (AP Photo/*The Canadian Press*, Jason Franson)

Pages 252–53: Duncan Keith (#2) of the Chicago Blackhawks hoists the Stanley Cup after the Blackhawks defeated the Philadelphia Flyers 4–3 in overtime to win the Stanley Cup in Game 6 of the 2010 NHL Stanley Cup Finals at the Wachovia Center on June 9, 2010, in Philadelphia, Pennsylvania. (Photo by Bruce Bennett/Getty Images)

Pages 278–79: Charlie Coyle (#3) of the Minnesota Wild skates during warm-ups with his stitches on display prior to Game 3 of the second round of the 2014 Stanley Cup Playoffs against the Chicago Blackhawks on May 6, 2014, at the Xcel Energy Center in St. Paul, Minnesota. (Photo by Bruce Kluckhohn/NHLI via Getty Images)

Pages 288–89: The Boston Bruins' Derek Sanderson (#17) and the Minnesota North Stars' Lou Nanne (#23) battle for the puck in the second period of their National Hockey League game on Thursday, December 14, 1973, at Boston Garden. Boston won the game, 4–2. (AP Photo)

Insert

Page 1: NHL Playoffs—the New Jersey Devils' Randy McKay (#21) with referee and sustaining injury, blood, after fight vs Buffalo Sabres, East Rutherford, NJ, 4/19/1994. (Photo by Al Tielemans/*Sports Illustrated*/Getty Images)

Page 2 (top): Equipment litters the ice as officials break up a fight between the Detroit Red Wings' Martin Lapointe, left, and the Colorado Avalanche's Eric Lacroix as Detroit's Brendan Shanahan, right, and Rene Corbet (#20) go at it during a third-period brawl in Game 4 in the Western Conference Finals series at Joe Louis Arena, Thursday, May 22, 1997, in Detroit. Detroit shut out Colorado, 6–0, and took a 3–1 lead in the series. (AP Photo/Tom Pidgeon)

Page 2 (bottom): Mike Ribeiro (#63) of the Dallas Stars is restrained by Kris Draper (#33) of the Detroit Red Wings after Ribeiro slashed goaltender Chris Osgood (not pictured) during Game 2 of the Western Conference Finals of the 2008 NHL Stanley Cup Playoffs at Joe Louis Arena on May 10, 2008, in Detroit, Michigan. The Red Wings defeated the Stars, 2–1, to set the series at 2–0 Red Wings. (Photo by Dave Sandford/Getty Images)

Page 3 (top): Tie Domi (#28) of the New York Rangers fights with Bob Probert (#24) of the Detroit Red Wings on February 9, 1992, at Madison Square Garden in New York, NY. (Photo by B Bennett/Getty Images)

Page 3 (bottom): Cam Neely of the Boston Bruins, right, tries to avoid a punch by Rick Tocchet of the Philadelphia Flyers, left, in the first period of an NHL game in Boston Garden, December 6, 1986. Both players were penalized for fighting. (AP Photo/Peter Southwick)

Page 4 (top): With blood on his face, Canadian linesman John D'Amico (1937–2005) calls for help as he wrestles Pierre Bouchard of the Montreal Canadiens to the ice after a fight during the Stanley Cup Finals, Boston, Massachusetts, May 21, 1978. In the background, a second official breaks up a fight between John Wensink (in white) of the Boston Bruins and the Canadiens' Gilles Lupien. Though Boston won the game, Montreal went on to win the series and the Cup four games to two. (Photo by Bruce Bennett Studios/Getty Images)

Page 4 (bottom): National Hockey League official Andy Van Hellemond tries to separate the New York Rangers' Steve Richmond (#41), left, and the Philadelphia Flyers' Rick Tocchet (#22), partly visible at right, during an NHL game at New York's Madison Square Garden, April 3, 1985. (AP Photo/Mario Suriani)

Page 5: Marc-Andre Bergeron (#47) of the Edmonton Oilers and Kris Draper (#33) of the Detroit Red Wings shove each other in the face during Game 1 of the Western Conference quarterfinals at Joe Louis Arena on April 21, 2006, in Detroit, Michigan. The Red Wings defeated the Oilers, 3–2, in double overtime. (Photo by Dave Sandford/Getty Images)

Page 6: The Florida Panthers' Dave Lowry and the Philadelphia Flyers' Shjon Podein are a tangle of legs as they square off along the Panthers' bench at the end of Game 3 in their Eastern Conference semifinal in Miami, Tuesday, May 7, 1996. (AP Photo/Phil Sandlin)

Page 7 (top left): The Detroit Red Wings' Kirk Maltby (#18) checks the Nashville Predators' Nick Spaling in the second period of an NHL hockey game in Detroit, Friday, January 29, 2010. (AP Photo/Paul Sancya)

Page 7 (top right): Terry O'Reilly (#24) of the Boston Bruins is helped over to the penalty box after being involved in a fight as Brad Park (#22) talks with the linesman during a Stanley Cup quarterfinal game against the New York Islanders in April 1980 at the Nassau Coliseum in Uniondale, New York. (Photo by B Bennett/Getty Images)

Page 7 (bottom left): Andrew Shaw (#65) of the Chicago Blackhawks stands on the handshake line after Game 6 of the 2013 NHL Stanley Cup Finals at TD Garden on June 24, 2013, in Boston, Massachusetts. The Chicago Blackhawks defeated the Boston Bruins, 3–2, to win the Stanley Cup. (Photo by Bruce Bennett/Getty Images)

Page 7 (bottom right): Patrice Bergeron (#37) of the Boston Bruins speaks to the media following a 2–1 double-overtime victory over the Pittsburgh Penguins in Game 3 of the Eastern Conference Finals of the 2013 NHL Stanley Cup Playoffs at the TD Garden on June 5, 2013, in Boston, Massachusetts. (Photo by Jared Wickerham/Getty Images)

Page 8: Doug Gilmour (#93) and Wendel Clark (#17) of the Toronto Maple Leafs skate on the ice during an NHL game against the New York Rangers on December 6, 1996, at Madison Square Garden in New York, NY. (Photo by B Bennett/Bruce Bennett Studios/Getty Images)